TIPS & TRICKS

How to use this book

501 Speed Sketches demonstrates how to draw cartoons using a quick drawing style, providing simple instructions and notations. This book is jam-packed with 501 cartoons to draw that will keep the budding artist busy for a long time.

There are three types of illustrations to tackle in **501 Speed Sketches**:

- a main illustration with instructions
- suggested variations on the main illustration
- other subjects to illustrate, with notations

Most sections begin with a main illustration accompanied by step-by-step instructions. This will help you understand what to look out for during the drawing process and how important it is to draw a cartoon in stages. The main illustrations will provide a great foundation for the other drawings in the chapter.

Suggested variations offer funny or unexpected alternatives to the main illustrations. Cartoons are all about stretching one's imagination and coming up with new ideas. This style of drawing will hopefully inspire you to create your own designs.

Most drawings feature simple, clear notations to guide you quickly to a successful result. The labels point out key things to watch for and provide a neat summary of the subject.

Throughout the book you will find references to the introduction to remind you of the fundamentals of drawing. Whenever you need a reminder of the basic techniques involved, you can refer back to this section.

The drawing style in **501 Speed Sketches** is a simple cartoon style based around shapes and clear, articulated line work, with shading and detail kept to a minimum. Shading and extra detail are not essential for a successful outcome – cartoons can look just as good completed with just simple line work. The level of shading you choose to apply is up to you. You will find guidelines about pencil work and shading on page 32.

The introduction will guide you through the fundamentals of drawing and will cover:

- head construction
- facial expressions
- action and poses
- body language
- hands and feet

- drawing animals
- designing a character
- perspective and 3D
- tips on pencil use and shading

HEAD CONSTRUCTION

Shapes, proportion, character and facial features

Although they might not be the first things a character designer will draw, the head and face define your character's personality. These often guide the way the rest of the body will be expressed.

In this section, we look at proportion, viewpoints, facial guidelines, different head shapes and using a variety of facial features to convey character.

Look at characters in books, comics or on TV and observe the variety of head shapes.

facial
guidelines

Character studies

When designing a character, it pays to begin with some studies. Straight-on, profile (side-on) and three-quarter poses are standard viewpoints from which we often see drawings of people. Drawing facial guidelines, like those shown above, helps you draw the facial features (eyes, nose, mouth) in correct proportion to the head.

The eyeline and browline will go higher or lower depending on the type of character. For example, the eyeline for a child will sit halfway down the face or lower, but for a monster with a big jaw, the eyeline will be much higher.

4

face cross

5

6

face cross

face cross

Face cross

Whether the head is straight on, tilted or otherwise, it's important to put in a face cross to help you gauge the position of the eyes, nose and mouth.

Head shapes

You can choose whatever shape you like to build your head from, but choose wisely.

A square, angular shape will give your character an edge and convey strength, while a round or oval shape will soften the character's look. Frankenstein (to the right) is a good example of this theory.

Play around with shapes and forms, change eye levels – and don't forget the face cross!

8 Bean shape   **9** Oval   **10** Triangle

11 Scared and nervous

A long, narrow shape forms the head. Eyes are close together and the mouth is low.

12 Cute and adorable

The head is a round and soft shape. Big eyes are halfway down the face.

13 Big and ugly

This big bruiser has a head that features large oval jowls that hold his aggressive mouth. His small eyes are high up.

Dressing a head

Once you've created your head, don't forget to dress it up with a crazy hairdo or hat! This will help to bring your character to life.

14

15

16

FACIAL EXPRESSIONS

The face

When working out whether a person is sad, happy or angry, we look to their face for confirmation. We've all heard the expression 'It was written all over his face.' There are many features to play with when bringing vivid expression to a face. The more we focus on or amplify those features, the more expressive the emotion will be!

Broad expressions, whether they are laughter or anger, stretch or pull the face a certain way. Give greater power to your expression by matching the character's head shape to its expression.

17 The eyes have it

Ovals or circles are mostly used for eyes, and their positioning is important. They can be close together or wide apart. Don't forget about eyebrows – they provide the accent to the eyes.

18 Mouthing off!

We all know the curved lines that represent a smile or a sad expression. Break open a simple smile line to open a mouth into laughter. Curl up a lip for disgust or reduce it all to a small oval for an expression of surprise.

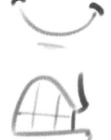

19 Being nosey

While noses don't have the same expressive qualities as the eyes or the mouth, they are certainly influenced by them – even more so on animals. Noses also help to define a character's personality.

Animal expression

Animals often have more prominent features than humans. This helps the artist create vibrant, expressive faces for them.

 **20**

 **21**

 **22**

 **23**

Exaggeration and amplification

As artists, we are not limited by concrete representation in the way that some other artistic disciplines are, such as photography. With cartooning we are only limited by our imagination. Set your character free and amplify their expression. Don't be timid – show them what you've got!

24 Pirate

Too much time at sea has made this pirate as crazy as a coconut! A bulbous nose, wild eyes and a toothless smile give him his personality. A three-quarter pose and a wonky hat help make him look even more insane!

GOOD

BETTER

GOOD

BETTER

25 Singer

This sassy lady's fantastic voice and great projection deserve a large mouth! Draw waves of dramatic hair and huge earrings springing from her head to give her a lot of dynamic energy.

26 Male model

Being a style icon is all about striking the right pose! This model's features are built from graphic shapes and angles. Super sharp!

GOOD

BETTER

ACTION AND POSES

Bring your character to life and make them move! The more dynamic the movement, the greater an angle the spine and limbs will be on. Build your action pose by drawing the spine first, then draw the lines through the shoulders, hips and feet. You'll be well on your way to getting a great action pose.

minimal angles

taking flight

spine line

lines through shoulders, hips and knees

steady movement

thrusting upwards, balanced by the arms

27

28

29

Basic poses

Before you can run, you need to walk. Take some time to get the balance right. The angle of the body increases with speed, but is balanced out by the extended limbs.

Standing   Walking   Running

Action animals

In the jungle or the ocean or on the open plains, animals are dancing and prancing to the beat of life. Build a strong, dynamic pose by drawing soft guidelines to start off with, then bring your active creature to life.

Movement: soft and dynamic

As with facial expressions, try to emphasise and amplify your character's pose. Avoid the static figure. Change your angles and skew the view. Why jog when you can sprint? Why jump when you can launch into space?

30

GOOD

BETTER

Space-mobile

A straight-on or side view isn't the best way to suggest speed. Create dynamic movement and action by drawing the space-mobile and rider from above, on an angle. The matching curves of the rider and space-mobile make the picture flow.

31

GOOD

BETTER

Soccer player

When you kick a ball, your whole body swings into action. Your legs launch forward and back and your arms splay out for balance. Avoid a stiff, rigid figure and employ flowing action lines.

32 Action stars

Superheroes are super for a reason. Whether it's super strength, speed or other special abilities, this guy doesn't sit around. Note the dynamic angles running from his back leg right through to his outstretched arm.

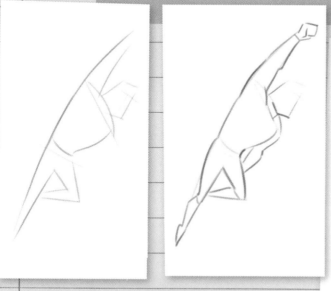

STRENGTH

SPEED

33 Monkey see, monkey do

Time to get some breakfast! This character has loose limbs and swings gracefully. Curves express his relaxed swinging movement.

AGILE AND ATHLETIC

BODY LANGUAGE

We don't have to rely solely on facial expression to tell us about our character. The body is the perfect platform to suggest specific emotions or characteristics.

34 Distressed

Body arching back with hands clasped to head.

35 Nervous

Buckled over with a frail pose, biting fingernails.

36 Elated

With his feet off the ground and his fist punching the air, this guy is excited!

Beans

Cartoon bodies are flexible and can be built from any shape. The bean shape is perfect. You can use this as a building block and develop the body language from there.

Fun stereotypes

Stereotypes are a heap of fun to play with and embody everything that is important about strong body language. Practise these guys to get off to a good start!

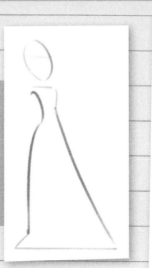

37 Starlet

Slinky and sophisticated – well, she certainly thinks so! This starlet wants to be noticed wherever she goes. Observe the sweeping curve of her back, the dress and the delicate arms in a model pose.

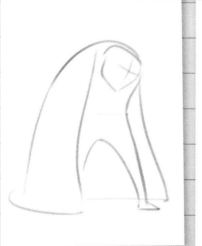

38 Professor Evil

Life hasn't been too good to Professor Evil. He's hunched over with a long, flowing cape and bowed legs. This guy is creepy to the core!

39 Klutz

He's always making a fool of himself by bumping into things and falling over. The klutz has an awkward pear-shaped body with skinny, floppy limbs and big feet.

Developing one character

A character can go through a range of emotions in a story, showing many different expressions. Learn how to adjust the character's body language according to how they feel. Maybe act out the expression in front of a mirror. Watch the way your body contorts and try to replicate it in your drawing.

40 Bored

Nothing on and nothing to do!

41 Elated

Great news!

42 Scared

Time to get out of here!

Play with the unexpected

Have fun with your characters and let them do the unexpected. Don't be boring! You'll find examples throughout the book. Whether it's a bulldog in a tutu, a gorilla smelling a flower or a dolphin at a bar, use interesting body language to express the personality of your character.

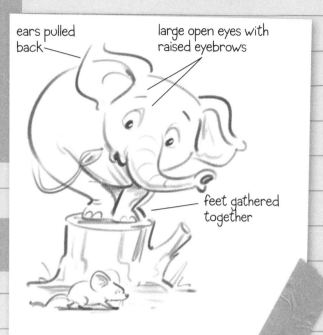

ears pulled back

large open eyes with raised eyebrows

feet gathered together

43 Scared elephant

confident walk

smile from ear to ear – 'Look what I can do!'

strong pose, chest out – 'This is easy!'

44 Strong boy

semi-reclined pose, sitting up in bed

focused – sad eyes with furrowed brow

45 Frankenstein reading

HANDS AND FEET

Hands and feet are one of the most important elements when drawing a character. Hands in particular can be very expressive and help to represent emotion. Whether they are pointing, gesturing or held in a tight fist, the hands often lead the way.

Hands and feet are the parts of the human body that people tend to have the most difficulty drawing. If you learn some of these basic fundamentals, you won't break out in a sweat when you come to draw them.

46

47

Basic hand construction

In cartoon or quick drawings, it's fine and sometimes preferable to draw fewer fingers. This simplifies the drawing process and lets your audience know they are in cartoon world!

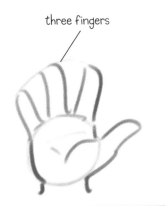

built from a ball

guidelines for length of fingers

three fingers

Basic hand poses

Cartoon hands almost always start with a ball shape, which will often define the palm or the back of the hand. From here, the finger shapes will be measured out, whether they are curled in or stretched out.

Note the position of the thumb and the point it springs out from. It works independently from the fingers.

48 Open hand

The open hand is drawn regularly in cartoons to show that a character is talking.

49 Making a point

It speaks for itself! Note how the last two fingers and the thumb curl in.

50 Gripping

A firm grip is often required. Whether the character is holding a newspaper, rope or stick, allow the fingers and thumb to wrap around the object.

Expressive hands

We know how expressive faces can be, but don't forget about hands! They may be very useful tools, but they are also a direct extension of a character's personality. Hands can be many things – strong and powerful, polite, or downright creepy looking. Give them soft lines or jagged edges. Make the fingers fine and slender, or bulk them up to indicate strength.

52 Crooked and creepy

51 Strong and powerful

53 Pretty and polite

Basic foot construction

To make sure your foot is well grounded, start with a horizontal line then build a wedge-like shape on top. Only when the form is developed should you add the details of the toes. Be careful not to make them look like fingers!

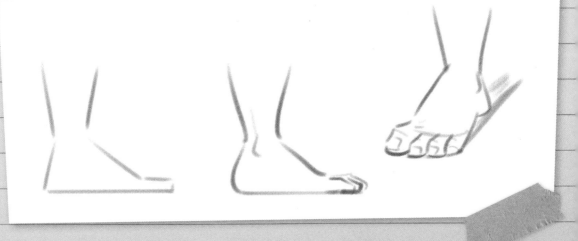

Human qualities in animal hands

Although in reality the paws, hooves and wings of animals are actually very different to humans, when drawing cartoons it pays to give them human qualities. This will make them very expressive and will add to your animal character's personality.

54 Cat

Cats' paws can still be expressive even if they are short and round. Top it off with some sharp claws.

55 Bird

The long feathers on a bird's wing can make for expressive hands. Be sure to include some ruffles or feather textures for effect.

56 Dragon

Dragons' feet are very different to humans' – for one thing, the heel is always raised – but the approach to drawing them can be similar, as seen above.

DRAWING ANIMALS

Drawing animals may seem difficult at first. There are four legs, floppy ears and tails to contend with. But at the heart of the process, drawing animals uses the same sort of construction as drawing humans.

Guidelines and shapes

Start with guidelines for the pose. Use basic shapes as your building blocks and then articulate the outline. First and foremost, give your animal character and personality. Apply what you know so far, but most of all, have fun!

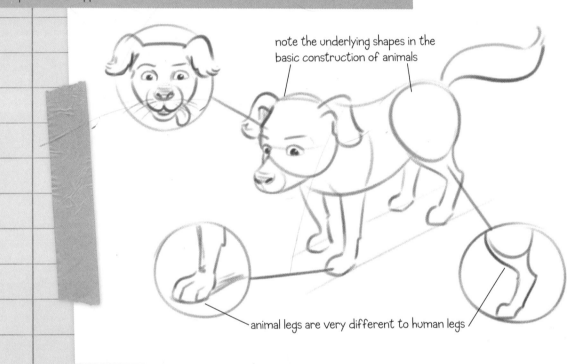

note the underlying shapes in the basic construction of animals

animal legs are very different to human legs

Bird   Dolphin   Horse

Giving animals human characteristics

Who said animals have to stay on all fours, be stuck in their web or remain perched in a tree? Give your cartoon creatures human characteristics and watch their personalities sing!

57
Leo the Leopard

Leo plays a mean bass!

58
Sammy the Spider

With all those legs he can play four octaves at once. Look at him go!

59
Tom the Toucan

Tom might be a smooth talker, but he also has a smooth voice. Give him a mike and he might never stop!

Expressive animals

Some of the most memorable cartoon characters in history are animals. Their prominent facial features give the cartoonist a lot of creative freedom. Make the most of them by giving your animals expressive faces.

60 Eyes

Fish

Frog

Tarsier

61 Noses, snouts and beaks

Pig

Elephant

Pelican

62 Ears

Rabbit

Dog

Donkey

Fur and feathers

Some might call them mere details, but fur and feathers, spots and stripes can go a long way in defining your cartoon animal as well as elaborating on their personality. So watch the fur fly, ruffle the feathers and spot the difference!

63

64

Observe the way each of these details is drawn. Some show loops, such as the feathers and scales, while the spots and stripes are loosely defined patterns with subtle shading.

DESIGNING A CHARACTER

Dr Jekyll or Mr Hyde?

When starting the drawing process, you decide what world your character lives in – be it fantasy, historical, sci-fi or the animal world. From there, you form a vision of their personality type. They could be a heroine, a villain, mysterious or just plain cute. Let these elements guide you as you take your ordinary Joe or June and turn them into something special.

65 Robot

66 Elvis

Ordinary guy

67 Pirate

68 Mafia boss

Exploring shapes and forms

When creating a character study, start with some basic shapes and lines. Keep your drawing style loose and try to find the essence of your character. When developing the form of your character's body, just see where your pencil takes you. Keep it simple. Once you feel you have something, add detail and areas of interest.

Choose a face

Invest time in drawing the face – you will reap the rewards. Refer to the pages on head construction (page 2) and facial expression (page 6) for guidance. Be inspired by your character's personality and match your design to that. Remember to be expressive and have fun.

Happy, friendly farmer

He has an oval-shaped head and large eyes which sit high up.

Strong man

He has a square jaw and thick neck.

Opera singer

About to break into song, she is poised to perform.

Hair, clothes and props

Now for the fun part! Knowing the personality of your character, add hair, props and clothing to help them fully express themselves.

69

Happy, friendly farmer

With the sun bearing down on him all day, the farmer needs a hat. The wheat is a playful gesture and also tells us what his crop is.

70

Strong man

The strong man's oh-so-serious look shows us he is fully focused. Got to lift more weight! No pain, no gain.

71

Opera singer

Reaching for the highest note takes a lot of effort. The opera singer has a wide mouth and expressive arms and her chest is out.

Exaggeration and amplification

Enjoy doing different things with your character to enhance their personality traits.

HAVE FUN WITH FORMS!

DRESS THEM UP!

DON'T BE DULL!

72
Space dog

An adventurous space dog will be proud and resolute. We know he can get the job done.

BE GRAPHIC!

FIND DYNAMIC ANGLES!

DO THE UNEXPECTED!

73
Funky singer

A funky singer moves to the beat and is lost in her song. Graphic shapes give an edge to her performance.

PERSPECTIVE AND 3D

When drawing objects on paper, it's important to give the correct impression of depth, width and length. This is where perspective comes in.

Perspective and skewed views

As an artist, you can depict volume and spatial relationships on a two-dimensional surface like paper. Objects will decrease in size as they get further away from the viewer. Perspective is particularly useful when drawing solid objects like houses, boats and cars. You can set off a series of perspective guidelines prior to starting your drawing. These lines will usually meet at a vanishing point on a horizon line.

Foreshortening

Skewed views involve perspective at work. They also highlight the phenomenon of foreshortening, where an object looks compressed when seen from a certain angle.

Looking up

A skewed view is seen from the ground looking up, which highlights our giant's size.

Close-up

A close-up of the head from the same viewpoint makes the giant's head look enormous.

From above

Now we see our giant from above, giving you the impression he isn't so big after all!

Creating 3D forms

Sketching two-dimensional forms is the basis of nearly everything we draw. Many times we have spoken about building with basic shapes. But once the drawing has been developed, it is nice to give it a bit of oomph and pop by making it look three-dimensional. This gives the impression of something solid, rather than flat. Using your pen or pencil, add some tone or graduation to one side of the object to achieve this.

 2D triangle to 3D hat form

2D circle to 3D sphere

2D square to 3D cube

2D teardrop shape to 3D bean

74 Putting it into practice

Shading and tonal rendering is not essential to make a great drawing. Some of the best drawings use only very simple, well-articulated line work. But if you want to go that extra step, don't be afraid to add some shading and extra accents to really lift your drawing off the page.

Pencil work

It is important to understand how best to use a pencil before you start. We recommend using a HB or 2B pencil. If you choose to use a black fineliner pen, the same grip would apply. Have a clean eraser ready to rub out any line work you no longer need. It also helps to have a sharpener and dish for shavings ready to go!

Pencil pressure lines

It's all about the pressure! Practise your pressure on a separate piece of paper before you begin drawing. In simple terms, a light pencil pressure gives you a light grey line, a medium pressure a medium grey line and a heavy pressure a dark grey line.

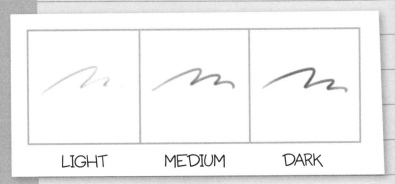

LIGHT   MEDIUM   DARK

Shading

If you choose to shade your cartoon, you need to understand the scale of shading. Look at the scale on the right. One end of the shading scale shows light grey tone, the middle shows medium grey tone and the end shows dark grey. Use the same pencil grip as above to achieve different tonal values; your pencil, however, should be held on a slight angle.

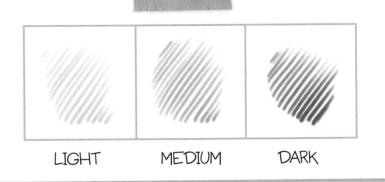

LIGHT   MEDIUM   DARK

This dragonfly is shaded using different examples from the tonal scale. Varied pencil pressure provides accents and added detail.

AMAZING ANIMALS

RAINING CATS AND DOGS

From elegant Siamese cats to beefy bulldogs, the world of cats and dogs is filled with varying personalities and unique features. Humans have always been drawn to them – their saggy jowls, floppy ears and big doe eyes. We pamper them, we marvel at their energy, and we laugh at their tricks. Where would we be without our pet companions?

75 Classic Dog

Here boy! This happy young dog has big eyes, a shiny nose and floppy ears. His tongue is hanging out and his tail is alert as he waits for a doggy snack.

1 Draw an oblong head and a muzzle. Follow with a curved body.

2 Add floppy ears and facial features. Draw his legs and an alert tail.

3 Draw pupils, whiskers and a collar. Define his furry outline and add shading. What a good dog!

76 Happy walking dog

ears are relaxed and forward

tail wiggles

tongue hangs out with a big smile

tag is moving, and front leg is lifted

TIP

To make your dog's tail wag, use lines to show that it is moving.

77 High jumping dog

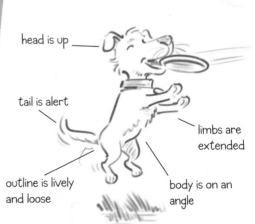

head is up

tail is alert

outline is lively and loose

limbs are extended

body is on an angle

78 Bulldog ballerina

A bulldog in a tutu is funny, because it's the complete opposite to his reputation as a tough dog! Big round shapes and a chubby outline give him his large form.

layered round shapes

floppy jowls

facing up

chunky arms

crinkly folds

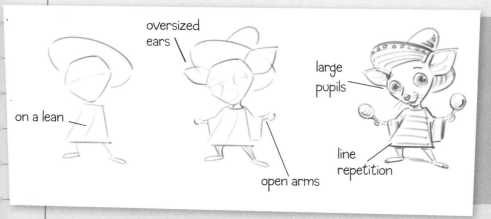

oversized ears

large pupils

on a lean

line repetition

open arms

79

Chihuahua

An oversized sombrero, big ears and bulging eyes give this little creature a cheeky personality. Drawing maracas adds a Mexican touch!

80 Intellectual terrier

Big furry jowls and a panting tongue show us his character. Add a scarf and glasses to make him look extra smart!

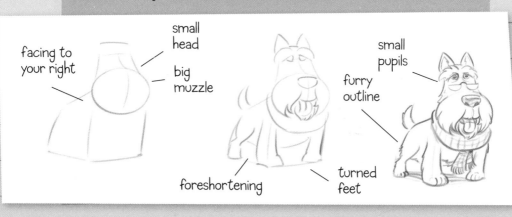

facing to your right

small head

big muzzle

small pupils

furry outline

foreshortening

turned feet

81 Classic cat

Purr! This cool, sleek young cat has big triangle ears and an alert tail. He's relaxed as he takes his time finding a spot for a nap, his bell jingling as he walks.

TIP

To draw a furry outline, use a line style that is loose and partly jagged. Notice how the outline changes from light to medium to dark. Changing the pressure of your pencil makes your outline fresh and lively.

1 Draw the head, followed by a curved body and skeleton legs.

2 Draw the details of his face, then define the body and add a tail.

3 Add pupils and other facial features. Now draw a collar and your cat will purr!

82 Human-like stance

Tail up, top hat tilted and a cheeky smile. When an animal is given an expressive pose it shapes their character! Meeow!

83 Human-like hands

Give your cat human qualities by drawing hands instead of paws! Now it's show time!

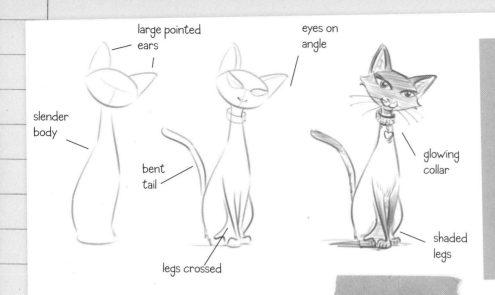

large pointed ears

eyes on angle

slender body

bent tail

glowing collar

legs crossed

shaded legs

84

Siamese cat

This cat is sleek and slender with great poise. Her aloof gaze and tilted head give her the air of a princess. A diamond-encrusted collar makes her a pretty kitty!

85 Cute kitten

A big head, large doe eyes, a petite body and a heart-shaped muzzle capture this animal's appeal. Eyes gazing at a playful butterfly set the scene and show its curious nature.

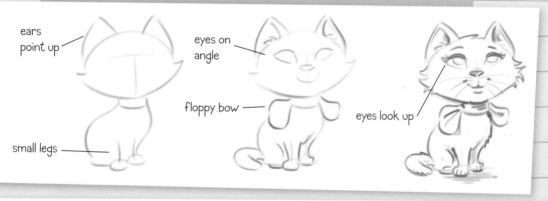

ears point up

eyes on angle

floppy bow

eyes look up

small legs

crown on angle

furry outline

bent tail

open mouth

underneath is flat

TIP

Check out Drawing Animals on page 22 of the introduction to learn more about giving animals human characteristics!

86 Reluctant lion king

This loafing lion has his head in his hands, his crown askew, a bored expression and a lazy pose. All of these elements make him appear disinterested.

JUNGLE JAM

What's that I hear? Trumpeting elephants taking a bath, frogs croaking, leopards roaring and birds chirping: it's a great cacophony of noise. It's a jam in the jungle! The jungle is home to some weird and wonderful creatures, from the big-beaked toucan to the little piranha with his gnashing teeth. Look, learn and listen. The jungle jam is in session!

87 Spouting elephant

This young elephant has a big round frame, floppy ears and a trunk like a hose. His favourite pastime is to spout water while he takes a bath!

1 Draw a rounded head and body. Add a thick, curved trunk that's thinner at the top. Draw the front legs and a baseline below.

2 Draw the mouth and trunk openings. Define the outline of the elephant's body, legs and trunk.

3 Draw the elephant's eye, hair and floppy ear. Add a tail and toenails. Lightly sketch the water.

89

88

90

Elephant This happy elephant likes to play and trumpet with laughter. But at the end of a fun-filled day he's tuckered out from all the activity. Now it's time to have a snooze!

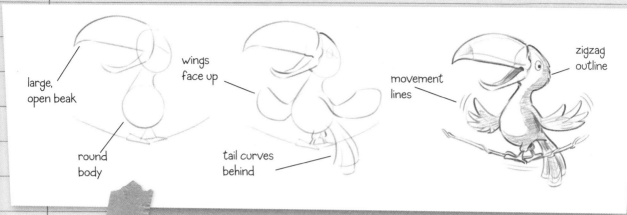

large, open beak

round body

wings face up

tail curves behind

movement lines

zigzag outline

91 Tightrope toucan

What a balancing act! This toucan likes to travel from tree to tree on a tightrope, making a croaking sound as he goes. His big open beak and feathery wings and tail help keep him balanced. He's a very clever acrobat!

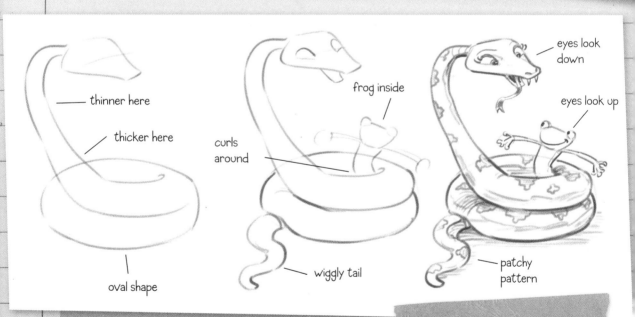

thinner here

thicker here

oval shape

curls around

frog inside

wiggly tail

eyes look down

eyes look up

patchy pattern

92 Friendly python

Who said pythons aren't friendly? This pretty python is keeping the little frog very cosy and warm with her thick, curled-up body. They are firm friends. Open your arms, frog. It's time for a hug!

93 Leopard

This serious leopard stands silently on a rock waiting for his prey; he's ready to pounce with his solid legs. His coat has a decorative pattern that highlights his form.

1 Draw the leopard's head, followed by his angular body. Draw curved rocks beneath, then sketch all of his legs.

2 Add pointed ears and thin shapes for the eyes. Define his nose, open mouth and body outline. Draw a curled tail and lines for his toes.

3 Draw pupils, sharp teeth and fur around his face. Shade a soft, circular pattern over his body. Add any other shading. Draw fine whiskers, and then add the plant behind him. Your leopard is on the prowl!

TIP

Check out Drawing Animals on page 22 of the introduction to learn more about drawing fur!

95

94

96

Frog leap

This frog is showing us an action sequence. He leaps from stationary to flying, then into a diving pose. It's all in the eyes, legs and arms. Check out the movement in the arms and legs between each step. His eyes look up, then down. Movement lines also enhance the action. Ribbit!

97 ## Piranha

This grumpy piranha has been waiting a long time for his catch of the day. His angular body, angry expression and oversized teeth show us his mood. Don't go near the water!

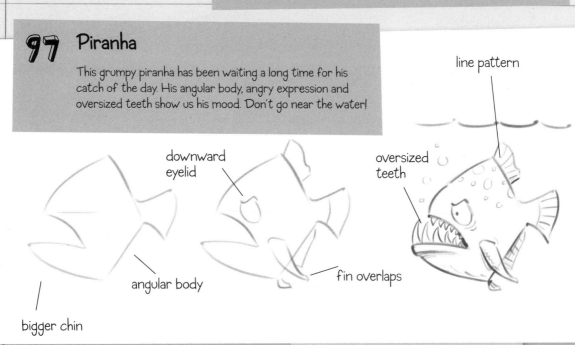

line pattern

downward eyelid

oversized teeth

angular body

fin overlaps

bigger chin

98 ## Surprise!

Uh-oh! This piranha has never seen his reflection before. What a shock! Now he understands why everyone runs at the sight of him!

BIRDS OF A FEATHER

As the saying goes, birds of a feather flock together. They also dance and puff out their feathers, sing sweet melodies and have a keen eye for food. Different birds symbolise different things. An owl represents wisdom, a flamingo symbolises beauty and grace, and an eagle signifies power and strength. With their different shapes and sizes and their curious natures, birds make for expressive drawing subjects.

99 Saluting eagle

Eagles are a symbol of power and strength; this one is no exception, with his puffed-out chest and big wings! He is at your service!

1 Draw the head and the rounded body, followed by the wing shapes.

2 Draw the beak on a straight angle. Form the hands, legs, feet and tail.

3 Define the eagle's feathered outline and draw the facial features. Sketch jagged lines for feathers and add shading. Now your eagle is ready to soar!

100

Human-like arms

You can give a bird's wings human qualities by lightly sketching a joint and muscle structure and human hand shapes. The positioning of the arms is also important. Focus on the angle and the viewpoint of the hands.

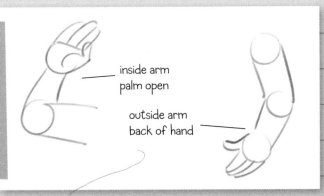

inside arm palm open

outside arm back of hand

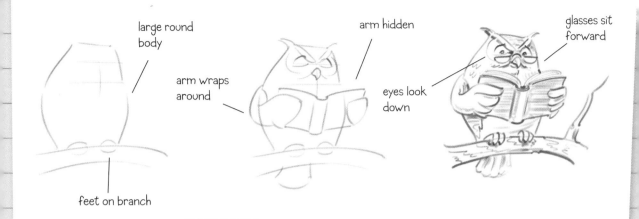

large round body

arm wraps around

arm hidden

eyes look down

glasses sit forward

feet on branch

101 Wise owl

This rotund bird perches for lengthy periods, watching the world go by and studying every detail. The glasses and the open book make him look wise and studious.

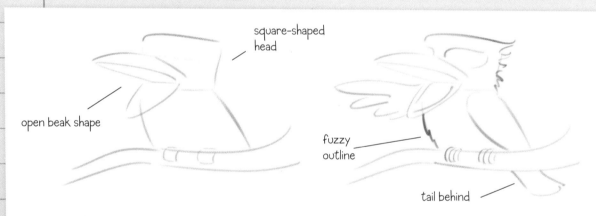

square-shaped head

open beak shape

fuzzy outline

tail behind

102

Cackling kookaburra

A wide-open beak and closed eyes give this performing bird its happy disposition. He is virtually bursting with laughter – his loud cackle can be heard for miles!

sound burst

wing over branch

dark shading inside

TIP

Check out Hands and Feet on page 18 of the introduction to learn about giving an animal character human qualities!

head looks up

musical notes

open, pointed wings

feathered outline

open legs

103 Little bluebird

This joyful little bird displays its happiness with open flapping wings as it lifts off the branch below. It also greets the day with a sweet, sweet song!

TIP

Beginning with a skeleton – made up of joints, bones and muscles – helps to create the overall form.

curved neck

beak points upwards

feathered outline

elevated leg

curled-up wings

TIP

Check out Drawing Animals on page 22 of the introduction to learn more about drawing feathers!

104 Dancing flamingo

This flamingo is like a tall and elegant dancing ballerina! It has a curvaceous neck, curled-up wings and long, slender legs. Its cheerful smile shows that it's really having a good time!

Beak shapes

When drawing a bird's beak, consider how the overall shape looks. Is it sharp, pointed or round?

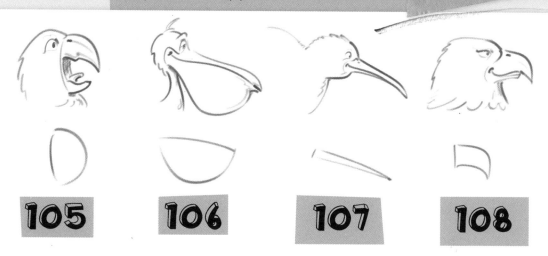

105   **106**   **107**   **108**

109

Greedy vulture

This greedy vulture is perched in a tree with his neck craned and beady eyes alert, awaiting his next meal. He holds a knife and fork, ready to swoop.

1 Draw an oval head with a bent neck. Sketch the vulture's collar and body, followed by his feet. Add a line for the branch.

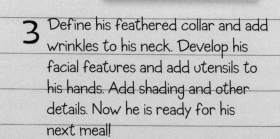

2 Add a crooked beak and furrowed brow line. Draw the wings with humanised hands. Sketch toes, a crooked branch and a tail behind.

3 Define his feathered collar and add wrinkles to his neck. Develop his facial features and add utensils to his hands. Add shading and other details. Now he is ready for his next meal!

HORSING AROUND

A horse can be many things – playful, intelligent, strong, fast, friendly and helpful. They are particularly known for their athletic prowess and their unwavering service to humans. Their long limbs and muscled physiques create striking poses and dynamic action lines. A racehorse is agile and sleek. A Clydesdale is powerful and strong. A Shetland pony is good-natured and friendly. Giddy-up!

110 Classic horse

What a beauty this horse is! This muscular, majestic beast stands firm and strong, with an alert posture and a confident expression. He is ready to compete!

1 Draw the head, muzzle and neck, followed by the curved, muscular body. Draw his front skeleton legs on an angle, and then add the back legs.

2 Form the shape of the body around the whole skeleton.

3 Define and darken the outline. Draw a flowing mane and tail. Add facial features and shading. Giddy-up!

112 Cartoon horse

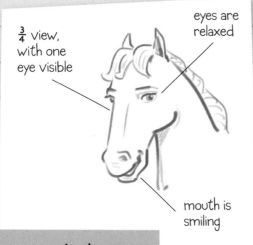

¾ view, with one eye visible

eyes are relaxed

mouth is smiling

open, expressive eyes

surprised expression, front-on pose

floppy mane

goofy mouth

111 A classic horse pose

TIP

Beginning with a skeleton – made up of joints, bones and muscles – helps to create a horse's muscular form.

113 Racehorse

A strong and arrogant pose shows off the importance of this horse! Crossed legs, a raised head and a perky tail all say 'Look at me!'

$\frac{3}{4}$ pose

skeleton legs

legs crossed

ears alert

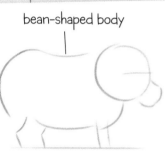

bean-shaped body

thick mane

eyes look down

114 Shetland pony

A relaxed and good-natured animal, this Shetland pony likes chilling out in the field. A floppy, overgrown mane and tail capture his friendly nature.

oversized muzzle and hooves

curved, open mouth

hairy hooves

115 Clydesdale

The Clydesdale is a tough animal that is able to pull heavy loads. His solid form and large hooves display his strength. He must get sick of working! Maybe that's why he looks surprised, and slightly annoyed!

INCREDIBLE CRAWLIES

The sheer mention of the words 'insect', 'snail' or 'spider' makes some people's skin crawl! Whether you find them creepy or not, these little creatures are truly incredible. Ants travel long distances in pursuit of food, spiders weave intricate webs and snails leave a long, silvery trail that maps their path. Insects can be angry, annoying, beautiful or musical, but their delicate and intricate features are a wonder to observe.

116 Musical praying mantis

This praying mantis is happiest when she perches on her leaf, serenading the other garden insects with her sweet song on the harmonica!

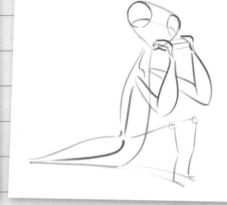

1 Draw the praying mantis' tilted head and its body, which is flat on the bottom. Draw its front legs on the same angle.

2 Draw the front arm, then the one behind. Add eyes and a harmonica between the hands. Draw a line down the backbone.

3 Draw antennae, pupils looking down and a line pattern on the body. Thicken the front legs, and then add the back legs. Draw detail on the harmonica and add musical notes. Now add shading and the wavy leaf. Your mantis is ready to perform!

TIP

Check out Designing a Character on page 26 of the introduction to learn more about character development!

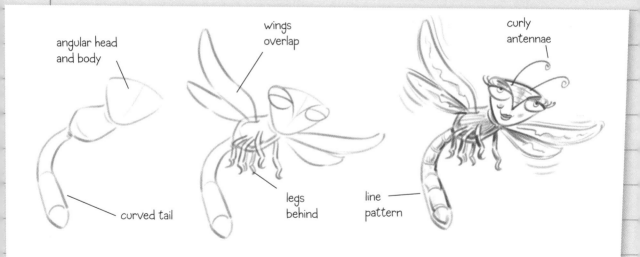

angular head
and body

wings
overlap

curly
antennae

curved tail

legs
behind

line
pattern

117 Dragonfly darling

The dragonfly is a beautiful creature of the sky. Delicate wings,
a long, fancy tail and big eyes make up this distinctive insect. You
can sometimes hear a buzzing sound as it zips by!

118 119 120 121

Insect shapes

Drawing bugs and beetles doesn't have to take time. Draw some simple and
quick insects by using basic shapes. The body shape forms the basis for each
cartoon. Then use lines to create legs and wings, circles for eyes and irregular
shapes for feelers and horns. Just add shading and you're done!

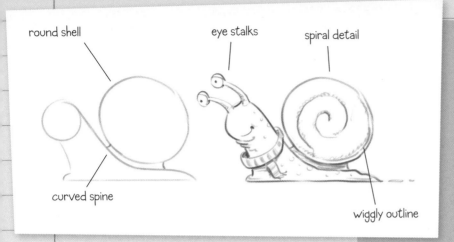

round shell

eye stalks

spiral detail

curved spine

wiggly outline

122

Slow snail

This slimy creature takes his time. His body is relaxed, his eyes are sleepy and his smile is content. The snail's body is wiggling slightly – this shows he is slowly moving.

round body

head overlaps

floppy hair

annoyed expression

draw front legs first

hairy body and legs

123 Terrible tarantula

This tarantula is like a sloppy, stubborn teenager. His hair is lank, his drink is dripping and his expression says, 'I don't care!'

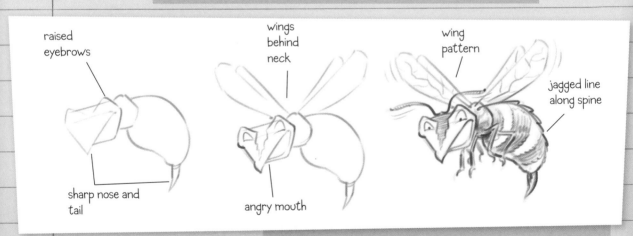

raised eyebrows

wings behind neck

wing pattern

jagged line along spine

sharp nose and tail

angry mouth

124 Angry wasp

His angry expression shows this wasp's aggressive nature. The bristling backbone, sharp nose and tail, and buzzing wings all show that he is ready to attack. Look out!

125 Super ant

Super strong, this ant can carry more than her own weight. She's happily part of the team, taking food back to the nest with her fellow worker ants.

1 Draw the ant's curved head and chest, and her round hips. Add her open legs and both sets of arms, with palms facing up.

2 Draw the rock shape sitting on top of the ant's palms. Thicken the width of her arms and legs. Add the eyes and mouth.

3 Darken and define the ant's outline. Draw a line pattern on her body and develop the facial features. Add antennae and shading. Now your ant can show her strength!

Extreme makeover

Transform a character's personality from old and grumpy to perky and well-groomed by drawing opposing features. Change their eyebrows from down to up, and their mouth from angry to happy. Change a pose from hunched to upright and a hairdo from messy to neat.

126 Angry, crotchety beetle

127 Happy worker beetle

ON THE FARM

The distant sound of clucking hens, mooing cows and bleating lambs tells us that the farm must be just over the hill. The animals that live there form one big raucous family, each with their own distinct personalities – from the soft and sensitive lamb to the gawky, greedy goat. Life is always busy on the farm. Cows need to be milked and eggs have to be collected. It's time to start the day. Cock-a-doodle-doo!

128 Chubby pig

This chubby pig is content with life on the farm; he's eagerly awaiting his next snack. He's been staying out of trouble: there's no mud in sight!

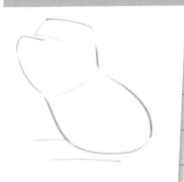  

1 Draw the pig's head and upturned snout. Add its rounded body, then draw two baselines underneath.

2 Draw two floppy ears and define the snout. Draw all the legs against the baselines.

3 Draw raised eyebrows and two happy, open eyes, looking up. Add a smile and a wiggly tail. Darken and define the pig's outline and apply shading where needed. Here, little piggy!

129 Scared pig

130 Bossy pig

Emotion and expression

Your happy pig on the farm can sometimes have a bad day! Occasionally he can be bossy or sometimes he might feel scared. Changing a character's expression and the positioning of their body parts can show their emotion. Note the differences between the eyes and mouths for these characters.

smaller leg behind

alert tail

hooves are larger

floppy fringe

woolly outline

131 Cute and cuddly lamb

Who doesn't love an adorable baby lamb? Just look at her cute and cuddly appearance – those floppy ears, her doe eyes and her soft, woolly coat. No wonder she won first prize at the show!

pointed tail

round body

open beak

feathered wings

wing is lifted

webbed feet

132 Waddling duck

A waddling duck is a curious sight! His round body, long neck, wings and webbed feet cause his body to shift from side to side as he walks. Can you hear him quacking in the distance?

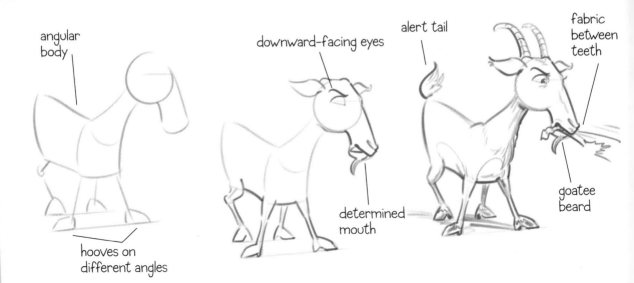

angular body

downward-facing eyes

alert tail

fabric between teeth

goatee beard

determined mouth

hooves on different angles

TIP

Check out Drawing Animals on page 22 of the introduction to learn more about animal construction!

133 Greedy goat

This goat is ready to eat everything in sight. His angular body, alert ears and tail and bracing pose show that he is determined to retrieve the fabric he's found. His firm gaze displays his greedy, stubborn nature.

rounded body

curled tongue

patchy pattern

crossed legs

thicken legs

swinging tail

134 Bluebell the cow

Bluebell is an adorable but lazy cow. She stands around the paddock chewing on grass and flicking away insects with her tail. Her patchy pattern makes her stand out from the crowd while she's waiting to be milked.

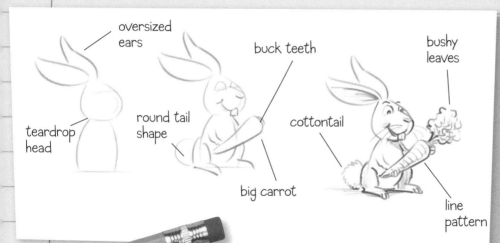

oversized ears

buck teeth

bushy leaves

teardrop head

round tail shape

cottontail

big carrot

line pattern

135

Classic rabbit

The classic features of this rabbit are his oversized ears, buck teeth and long whiskers. His puffy cottontail sets off the look as he gets ready to munch on his carrot!

136

Easter bunny

Another classic animal character is the Easter bunny. This one has been humanised with long arms and legs and human-like hands. His loose body pose, floppy ears and big teeth and smile reveal his goofy nature!

137

Family portrait

Roosters, hens and their chicks all live together in a big chicken coop, like one big happy family! Life's good for Mr and Mrs Rooster and their chick. There's nothing like a family portrait to capture the moment! Say 'Cheese!' This one's for the photo album.

DEADLY AND DANGEROUS

Deadly and dangerous creatures live in all parts of the world. Humans fear them, and try to keep their distance. With their sharp teeth, poisonous venom or menacing size, just the presence of these creatures is enough to send a shiver down your spine! So take note of the croc signs, stay close to the shore, and be sure to wear long pants in the jungle: you never know what might be lurking nearby!

138 Great white shark

One of the most feared creatures in the sea, this massive shark preys on seals (and sometimes people!). He looks vicious with his sharp teeth and angry expression.

1 Draw the curved, irregular-shaped body, with a pointed tail and a big opening for the mouth.

2 Add curved fins and develop the tail shape. Draw bumpy eyes and a line inside the mouth.

3 From the front, draw sharp teeth inside the mouth. Draw his angry eyes, then add further detail and shading to his body. Now quick – swim for shore!

139

GOOD

Exaggerating emotion

Use everything available to you to express a particular emotion – all of the body parts are at your disposal. To draw an emotion effectively, you need to over-exaggerate expressions to give your cartoon greater impact. This great white shark is a real scaredy cat!

BETTER

140

141 Death adder

The name 'death adder' says it all! This deathly creature is known for his thick, striped body and long fangs. He looks angry – you'd better keep your distance!

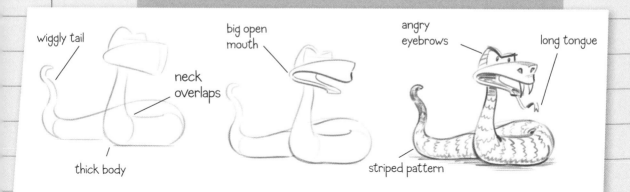

wiggly tail

big open mouth

angry eyebrows

long tongue

neck overlaps

thick body

striped pattern

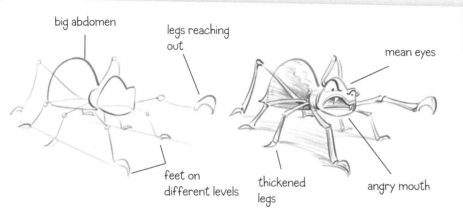

big abdomen

legs reaching out

mean eyes

feet on different levels

thickened legs

angry mouth

142

Black widow

This scary and venomous spider is known for her large abdomen and long, pointed legs. She looks ready to attack. Watch out for those sharp fangs!

143

Creating a sense of humour

Animals are known for their different personalities and qualities. Humans see death adder snakes and black widow spiders as scary. When drawing cartoons, surprise people by sketching something unexpected. Imagine a spider scared of heights, or snake that is afraid of humans. That really is funny!

144

145 Tiger

This fierce beast is showing his angry side with a forward-leaning pose, strong, bracing front feet and a straight, angled back. His menacing teeth and jagged tail show that he is ready to pounce!

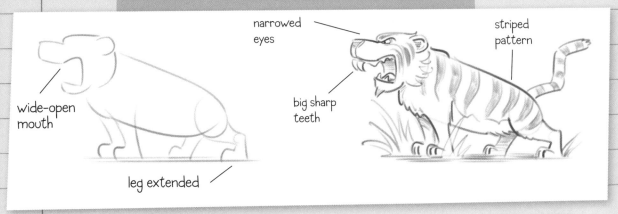

narrowed eyes

striped pattern

wide-open mouth

big sharp teeth

leg extended

146 Scorpion

A fearsome predator, this arthropod has a curved, segmented back, grasping pincers and a sharp stinger. He is on the attack – watch out for those fangs!

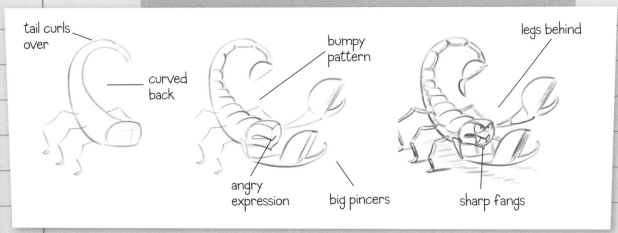

tail curls over

bumpy pattern

legs behind

curved back

angry expression

big pincers

sharp fangs

147 Surprised tiger

148 Confident scorpion

Not so deadly and dangerous

Imagine how these deadly animals would look if they were not so dangerous. Draw your tiger looking surprised instead of looking fierce, or your scorpion being confident instead of menacing. Have fun exploring different poses and expressions.

149 Super Croc

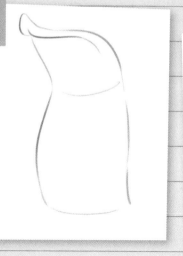

1 Draw a curved body shape with a curved tip for the croc's nose.

2 Add bumps for eyes, and then draw muscular arms with curled hand shapes. Draw the bumpy outline of the legs, and add a pointed tail. Draw the lines for the water.

3 Draw the croc's eye, his sharp teeth and the bumpy scales down his back. Draw a line pattern down his chest and on the tip of his tail. Add details and shading. Now presenting ... Super Croc!

150

Running scared

This croc is not like other crocodiles. He has a fish phobia! He went from Super Croc to super scared, thanks to the nasty nipper on his tail. Look how his tail and legs are lifted off the ground and his hands shoot forward. He's sprinting across the water in absolute terror!

PRECIOUS PRIMATES

There's a lot of monkey business going on in the jungle. Some of the precious primates are swinging from tree to tree, showing off as usual. Others are just aping around, picking flowers and sipping tea in the jungle garden. These fun-loving primates sure know how to enjoy life! A dancing baboon and a gibbon playing the bongos set the party atmosphere. It's time to join in the fun!

151

Gorgeous gorilla

Walking around the forest on her knuckles, this powerful gorilla has been studying the local flora. She's not interested in scaring the other animals: she wants to smell the flowers!

1 Draw the gorilla's head on an angle, followed by her arm. Sketch her angled chest and curved back leg.

2 Draw the gorilla's facial features and her bent arm holding a flower close to her face. Add her other leg, then define her fingers and toes.

3 Define the furry outline and add the pupils. Add petals to the flower, and shading around the gorilla's body. Draw the ground and plant. What a nice gorilla!

Gorilla at large

This gorilla is soft at heart and loves nature. But if anyone gets too close to her special flowers, she can lose her cool. Look at those angry expressions. She's not happy!

152   ## 153

154 Musical gibbon

Playing the bongos is this gibbon's preferred pastime. His long, slender limbs, fingers and toes make him the perfect bongo player. See how content he looks? He's in a really happy groove!

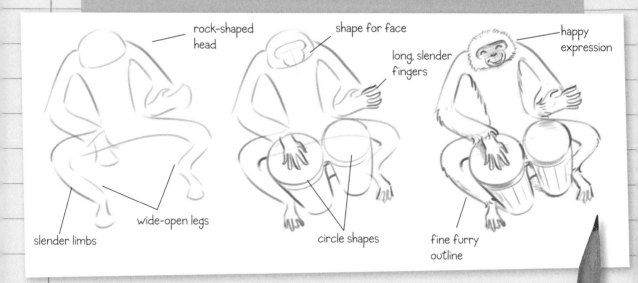

rock-shaped head

shape for face

happy expression

long, slender fingers

slender limbs

wide-open legs

circle shapes

fine furry outline

Cheeky little monkeys

These fun-loving monkeys like swinging from tree to vine. Their light, agile frames allow them to flip around like acrobats. Their bodies are small and their limbs are long and thin. Look at the simple shapes and curves at work when you go to draw them.

155

156

157 Civilised orangutan

How very civilised! Who knew that orangutans were partial to a cup of tea? This hairy beast with an oversized body and long limbs is content to chill out on the forest floor.

1 Draw the orangutan's chest and round tummy. Add the upper arms and the leg shapes, and then draw in the slightly bent feet.

2 Draw the orangutan's head below its shoulders. Add his forearms, and his hands, which are holding a cup and saucer.

3 Draw his small eyes, mouth and nose. Define his furry outline. Add fingers and toes. Pay attention to the positioning of his feet. Anyone for tea?

TIP

Check out Hands and Feet on page 18 of the introduction to learn more about character development!

158 Jiving baboon

Baboon is jiving and grooving to the sounds of the jungle. Look at his extended arms and feet lifting off the ground. His smiling face and curly tail show that he is having a really good time!

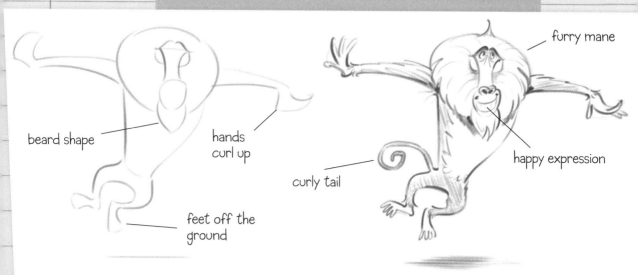

furry mane

beard shape

hands curl up

curly tail

happy expression

feet off the ground

Expressive faces

This chimpanzee has a range of expressions. Note the differences between these four emotions. It's all in the mouth and eyes. Look at how his face extends down when he is happy and surprised. You could use these same expressions when drawing humans, too!

159 Sad

160 Happy

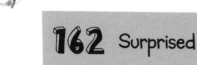

161 Angry

162 Surprised

FANTASY

FAIRYTALE FUN

'Once upon a time' is a story beginning that we are all familiar with. It is the opening line of many wondrous fairytales. Reading fantasies about royalty, talking animals, mystical beings and trickery takes us to a magical place. Let your mind run free and have fun with fairytale characters. Meet an evil queen, a dashing prince and genie in a bottle. See where the journey takes you!

163 Cinderella

Cinderella is escaping from the ball. It's a few minutes before midnight. She must run to meet her pumpkin carriage before the magic spell wears off and she turns back into a servant. Oh no! She's lost her glass slipper!

1 Draw Cinderella's bell-shaped skirt on a slight angle. Add her chest, then her head and neck.

2 Draw her hair and headdress. Add the puffy fabric around her waist then her thin arms. Now draw her slipper.

3 Draw her facial features over the cross. Define her hair and headpiece. Work your way down her body, adding the details of her gown. Softly draw the steps, the lost slipper and her wand. Cinderella, your carriage awaits you!

Ugly sisters

These sisters are snooty, snobby and grumpy! Look at their exaggerated facial expressions – they all look very annoyed. Their eyebrows are raised and their mouths are frowning. Observe the differences between their head shapes before you begin to draw.

164

165

166

TIP

Check out Designing a Character on page 26 of the introduction to learn more about exaggeration!

167 Fairytale castle

What a picturesque sight! A castle with tall towers, cone-shaped rooftops and decorative turrets are what fairytales are made of. The flags flapping in the wind help to set the scene.

cone shapes

turrets

flags moving

square shapes

168 Fairy godmother

A plump fairy with a blissful expression, this godmother is happy granting wishes all day long! She is a jolly personality with a round figure. Her arms look like two pointy wings.

pointy shapes

blissful expression

big round shapes

wavy pattern

169 Fairytale prince

This dashing prince is ready to save the day; he's on the lookout for a damsel in distress! His strong pose, flowing cloak and armour show he's ready to perform many acts of gallantry.

1 Draw the prince's angular body with his legs on an angle. Draw his head looking to the side and add his arm and face cross.

2 Build the shape of his form around the skeleton. Work your way down from the head, adding his hair and shield as you go.

3 Draw his face over the cross. Add his cape, belt and pointed sword. Define his costume and sword. Draw his boot and glove. Lightly shade his figure and the prince will be ready to save you!

Different scenarios

The fairytale prince doesn't just stand around looking princely all day long. There is so much more to him than that! He goes into battle, protects the kingdom from evil and is an excellent horseman. Try drawing the prince in two different scenarios.

170

171

172 Aladdin

Ready for a ride on a magic carpet? Aladdin will take you anywhere you want to go. He's surfing the carpet through the air, using his arms for balance. Whoosh! Off he goes!

TIP Check out Action and Poses on page 10 of the introduction to learn more about soft and dynamic movement!

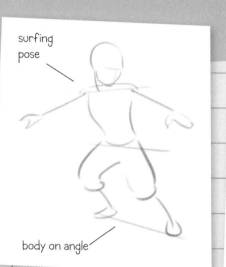

surfing pose

body on angle

whoosh lines

curled carpet

173 Genie

Rub the teapot and the genie will venture out in a trail of smoke. He is big and jolly, ready to grant you your three wishes. As he nods his head, magic glows around him like a light!

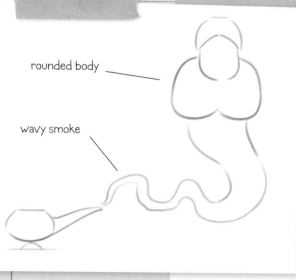

rounded body

wavy smoke

big smile

crossed arms

glow lines

WONDERFUL WIZARDS

Imagine if you were a wizard, living in the wonderful world of magic! A book of spells would be your guide to dealing with good and evil. You could recite powerful incantations to undo wicked spells and your wand would be your weapon! Picture yourself harnessing the healing power of ancient herbs to cure the sick, and having the power to control fire-breathing dragons! The world of wizards is just waiting to be explored.

174

Classic wizard

Wizards delve into the mystical art of magic to master the elements of nature. This wizard is all-powerful and acts as the guardian of his kingdom.

1 Draw the curved jaw of the wizard and add a face cross. Sketch the curved brim of his hat and add the pointed top that bends over. Draw the shape of his cloak.

2 Draw his hair and wavy beard. Add the sleeves of his cloak, with the one on your left at the same angle as his shoulders. Draw both of his arms.

3 Draw a serious expression over the face cross, then draw his staff. Define his fingers and draw two zigzags for the bolt of light. Define the details of his hat, cloak and beard. Add shading and the rock and mountains. Pure wizardry!

It's magic ... gone wrong!

Putting your character in a laughable situation adds humour to a picture. Your wizard is supposed to be a master of magic, but this time it's gone horribly wrong. He's messed up his spell and now he's paying for it!

175 Casting a spell

176 Oops!

177 Wizard's apprentice

This apprentice is learning the craft of magic from a masterful wizard. Ancient secrets of spell-making are being passed down to her. She is off to the forest to find herbs to concoct a powerful potion.

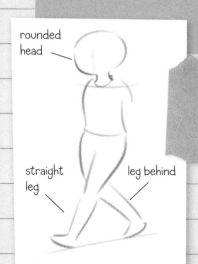

rounded head

straight leg

leg behind

bob haircut

cloak over shoulders

hand inside

face over cross

staff in hand

178 Goblin

This grumpy goblin is out to make a ruckus. He's an ugly creature with large ears, rotten teeth and a wart on his nose. He is fiercely loyal and will protect his master at any cost!

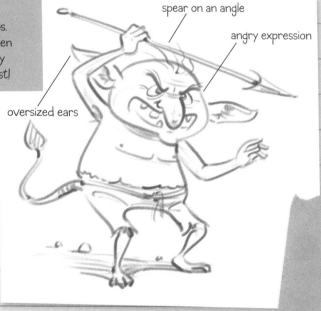

spear on an angle

angry expression

oversized ears

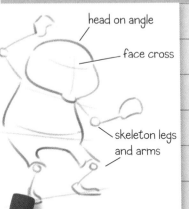

head on angle

face cross

skeleton legs and arms

179 Change up!

What's got into our naughty goblin? He must be under some kind of spell. Here he is gently patting a bird. Isn't it fun to play with a character's personality? It's OK to let your grumpy goblin be nice for a day.

180 Dragon

This strong, fire-breathing dragon is feared throughout the kingdom, with a reputation for showing no mercy. The knights of the realm have tried to capture him, but to no avail.

1 Draw the dragon's bell-shaped head. Sketch his curved neck and body. Add his front legs. Draw his smaller back leg and tail trailing behind.

2 Draw his eyes, open mouth and beard. Sketch frills either side of his eyes, then add his horns above. Add a pointy shape to his tail and draw claws on his feet.

3 Draw his angry eyebrows and eyes. Define his frills and nostrils, then draw scales down his back and tail. Lightly draw the shape of the flame. Add shading and further details to his skin. Fire away!

Young blood

This fun-loving teenage dragon has two pastimes. Whether it's catching some zzzs or listening to his music player, his wings take him wherever he wants to go! Try drawing your young dragon in another pose.

181

Sleeping dragon

182

Music-player dragon

183

Merlin

A powerful wizard with supernatural abilities, Merlin is destined to serve King Arthur and protect the castle of Camelot. With magic like no other, he is able to defend the realm from harm.

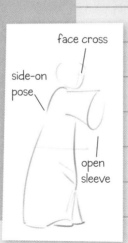

side-on pose

face cross

open sleeve

pointed hat

open palm

arm behind

star and moon pattern

burst of light

long, wavy beard

184 Sword in the stone

As legend has it, Merlin used his magic to place a sword in a stone. Whoever could pull the sword from the stone was the rightful King of England. Arthur Pendragon was the man who retrieved the sword.

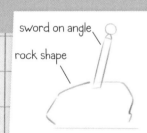

sword on angle

rock shape

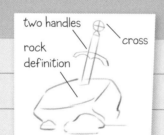

two handles

cross

rock definition

pattern on handle

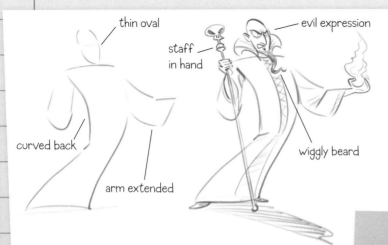

thin oval

staff in hand

evil expression

curved back

arm extended

wiggly beard

185

Evil sorcerer

This evil sorcerer is out to take control of the kingdom. He uses his wicked spells to wreak havoc, causing people to live in fear. His goal is to make the king disappear!

TIP

Check out Facial Expressions on page 6 of the introduction to learn more about drawing noses!

MYTHICAL CREATURES

Myths and legends are religious or supernatural in nature, and seek to explain different aspects of the world, such as how natural phenomena came to be. These stories have been part of human history for centuries. The creatures in these myths and legends are often a mix of human and animal and possess great powers. Whether it is a one-eyed Cyclops, a striking griffin or a beautiful mermaid, they are fascinating creatures to draw.

186 Cyclops

This gigantic one-eyed creature was born out of Greek mythology. He was one of the first blacksmiths and it is believed that volcanoes formed because of his underground work. The Cyclops is said to have given the god Zeus his lightning and thunder.

1 Draw his head on an angle, then sketch his big, rounded body. Draw his solid, muscular legs, with the one on your right lifted off the ground.

2 Add a face cross. Starting at his shoulders, draw his solid, muscular arms and big hands. Sketch the club in his hand, and his loincloth.

3 Draw his angry facial expression over the cross. Add his pointed ears and horn then create his fingers and toes. Darken and define his muscular form. Draw his cuffs and the spikes on his club. Lightly draw the rocky environment. Cyclops is on the warpath!

Break away!

Draw your Cyclops in opposing scenarios. Break away from his typical angry stereotype and show his softer side. Look! Our friend has stubbed his toe and is crying in pain! Imagine him as a baby – how cute!

187

188

189 Minotaur

This monster is half-man, half-bull. He lives in a labyrinth maze on the island of Crete. His huge, muscular form and large horns make him a beast to be reckoned with! He also has a terrifying reputation for eating human beings!

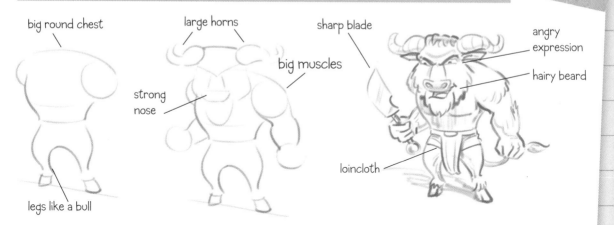

big round chest

large horns

sharp blade

angry expression

big muscles

hairy beard

strong nose

loincloth

legs like a bull

190 Griffin

This legendary creature has the head and wings of an eagle and the body of a lion. He is majestic and powerful and is known for guarding priceless treasures. When flying, his big, strong wings propel him into the sky.

bird-shaped head

lion-like body

big sharp beak

lion ears

large wings

191 Centaur

A strange beast, the centaur is part human, part horse. Centaurs are strong and quick in battle. They can sometimes be very hostile towards humans. Zeus would often send them to punish those who offended him.

looking up

curvaceous body

arms in line

horse's legs

hair moving

bow in hand

raised tail

192 Unicorn

These white, majestic animals are admired for their beauty and known for their magical horn. The horn itself can cure any poison. Unicorns are mysterious creatures that can only be found by those of great virtue and honesty.

1 Draw a round head with a muzzle. Sketch the unicorn's curved neck and chest followed by its belly and hind legs. Add the front legs.

2 Draw the form of the unicorn's legs and hooves. Darken and define their muscular outline and the shape of the muzzle. Lightly sketch the horn shape.

3 Develop the unicorn's eyes, nostrils and mouth. Draw the horn pattern and add the light, flowing mane running down its back. Sketch a puffy, alert tail. Add shading and the ground below. Pure magic!

Variations – different ages

From foal to young horse, try drawing your unicorn at different ages. A baby unicorn is cute – small in stature with oversized hooves. A young unicorn is more developed in appearance, yet slim, with an angular face and big eyes.

193 Baby Unicorn

194 Young Unicorn

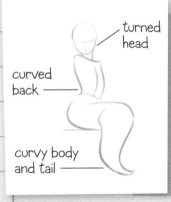

turned head

curved back

curvy body and tail

195 Mermaid

The mere sight of a mermaid can send sailors mad. Her beautiful appearance can be simply spellbinding, making men swoon. She is a fine swimmer, using her big tail to propel her through the water. She has shiny, wavy hair and her seated pose perfectly highlights her curvy body. Truly stunning!

hair texture

scale pattern

tail in water

wavy hair

thin arms

big tail

196 Medusa

This frightful looking creature is classified as a Gorgon. Once a beautiful goddess, Medusa was turned into a monster by a jealous counterpart. Her silky hair was replaced by hissing snakes. If you look directly at her, you'll turn into stone!

TIP

Check out Facial Expressions on page 6 of the introduction to learn more about expressions!

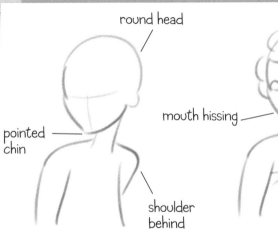

round head

pointed chin

mouth hissing

shoulder behind

snakes overlap

angry expression

CLASSIC MONSTERS

Check under your bed. Lock your doors and windows. There are monsters on the loose! Zombies are groaning, Frankenstein's moaning, and a werewolf is howling at the moon. You may think monsters are a myth, but seeing the giant footprints of Bigfoot or a werewolf is sure to send a shiver up your spine. You can run, but you can't hide!

197 Zombie

The zombies are coming for you! They are the dead that have been brought back to life by the power of mysticism. They escape their graves in the darkness of night, digging their way out through the dirt. Run!

1 Draw a round head and an angular chin. Add a face cross and neck. Draw the body with a baseline beneath. Add arms and legs.

2 Starting at his head, work your way down, drawing the form of his body around the skeleton.

3 Draw a menacing look over the face cross. Add his wavy hair and define his ears. Draw his long, claw-like fingers. Sketch his shoes and darken his outline. Once you add shading, your zombie will be on the prowl.

TIP Check out Action and Poses on page 10 of the introduction to learn more about action and power!

198

199

Drama and sequence

To add drama to your drawing, create a sequence that shows different stages of a story. Observe the two stages to the left: they show a close-up and the place the story is set in.

200

Frankenstein

This freakish creature was born from a science experiment gone wrong! A blocky head, oversized arms and body, and a goofy expression make this monster one to avoid.

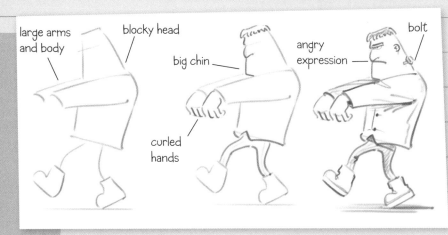

large arms and body

blocky head

big chin

angry expression

bolt

curled hands

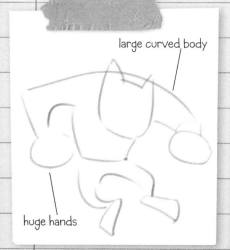

large curved body

huge hands

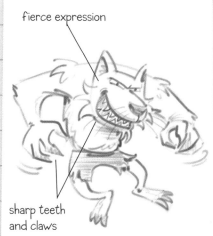

fierce expression

sharp teeth and claws

201

Werewolf

This monster shape shifts from human to werewolf when there's a full moon. His huge, muscular form is bursting out of his clothing. His fierce expression and oversized body tell you just how scary he is.

202 Mummy

Back from the dead, this mummy is sure to spook the locals! He is wrapped from head to toe in bandages. With his arms and leg extended, he's out to get you!

body on angle

leg lifted

arms extended

wrapped in bandages

203 Godzilla

A destructive reptilian monster, Godzilla rampages through the city, leaving a trail of destroyed buildings in his wake. Head for the hills – this gargantuan radiation-breathing creature is coming your way!

1 Draw Godzilla's triangular-shaped head and large curved body. Add his thick legs and fat, curved tail.

2 Create his open mouth, and then add bumps for his eyes and nostrils. Draw his small, thin arms.

3 Draw radiation coming from his mouth and add his sharp teeth and angry eyes. Form his sharp claws and draw bumpy scales down his back. Sketch the boat in his hand and add dripping water. Define his shape and add water and shading. Now run for your life!

204 Bigfoot

Watch out if you're camping in the mountains! You wouldn't want to find yourself in Bigfoot's path: look at the size of his massive fists and limbs!

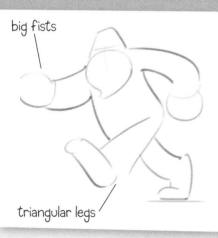

big fists

triangular legs

fierce expression

hairy linework

205 Loch Ness Monster

Uh-oh! This Scottish fisherman is about to get the surprise of his life! He's certainly not expecting to find a huge water monster snaking through the loch.

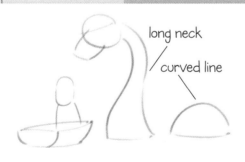

long neck

curved line

evil expression

spiky scales

legs

Different shaped heads

Look at these head shapes. Straight angular lines or curved lines can change a character's expression. Decreasing or increasing the size of a subject's jaw can indicate their character type.

206 Block   # 207 Hairy   # 208 Skull

TIP

Check out Head Construction on page 2 of the introduction to learn more about head shapes!

CREATURES FROM ANOTHER PLANET

Do you believe there is life on other planets? It's an interesting possibility to contemplate! If creatures from other planets visited our world, what would they look like? What language would they speak? Would they be friendly or fierce? Let your imagination run free by delving into this weird and wonderful world.

209

Escape from Earth

This creature is leaving Earth in a big hurry! He was supposed to be on a fact-finding mission, but he didn't like what he saw. Humans are really weird!

1 Draw the eye-shaped base of the ship. Sketch the creature's head above, with a surprised open mouth. Add his thin neck and body then add the circle above.

2 Draw his three eyes and the line inside his mouth. Add his collar, the seat and the steering wheel. Draw his front then back arm, and the spaceship's dome.

3 Draw his spiky hair, pupils and long tongue. Add the ship's three legs and the 'whoosh' lines behind. Draw and shade any further details over the spaceship and then off he goes!

210

Fun and humour

Forget a polite dinner; these creatures prefer a feast of sludge and worms. It's their favourite meal of the week and they are salivating over it! Anything's the go when drawing things from outer space. Yum!

211 Friendly

He's approachable, happy and fascinated by humans. His massive bug-like eyes, antennae and frog-like fingers make him look cute and friendly.

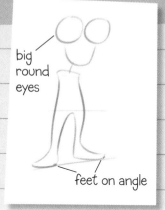

big round eyes

feet on angle

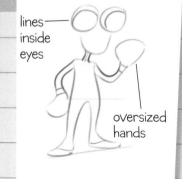

lines inside eyes

oversized hands

big smile

frog fingers

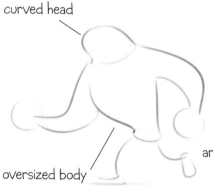

curved head

cloud-like pattern

oversized body

arrowhead-shaped tail

212

Menacing

This creature has sharp claws, rotting teeth and a devilish tail. His small legs and oversized body help to exaggerate his menacing appearance. The unusual cloud-like pattern on his body adds to the look.

213 Scared

This weird octopus-like creature is a bit creepy with his double noses and mouths, but humans actually frighten him! He looks alarmed and he's using his tentacles to help him run as fast as he can!

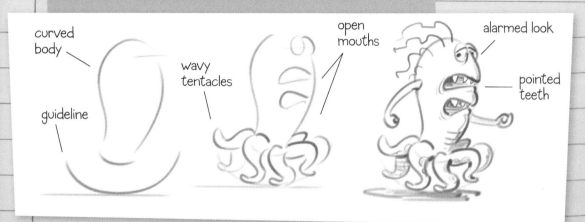

curved body

wavy tentacles

open mouths

alarmed look

pointed teeth

guideline

SPACE INVADERS

Launch yourself through the stratosphere and drift amongst the planets and stars. Land at your space station, where robots will tend to your every need. Grab a ray gun and get ready for battle with enemies from other planets. Jump into your spaceship and zip into the cosmos!

214

Spaceship captain

The leader of the space mission, this dependable captain makes all the important decisions. As his spaceship explores the universe, the crew relies on his knowledge of the galaxy and beyond. Computer! Set the coordinates!

1 Draw a big chest shape with angled shoulders. Draw thick legs at two different lengths on an angle.

2 Draw the head shape and the front arm leaning across the body. Draw the arm behind and the top of his boots, and add a curved line for the floor.

3 Draw his wraparound glasses and his strong facial expression. Draw his hair and his ear. Add the details of his uniform, then define his boots. Draw the curved shape of his computer console. Add shading and your space captain will be ready to take you to another planet!

The crew

215

Frontline officer

Tough, agile and ready for battle. She's there to protect the crew and keep enemies at bay.

216 Engineer

The engine-room operator. Solves maintenance issues and keeps the ship running smoothly.

217

Tech nerd

Oversees data, statistics and coordinates. When it comes to missions, he solves problems using his superior mathematical knowledge.

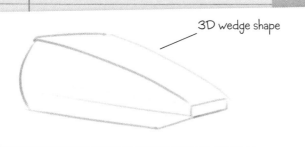

3D wedge shape

218 Spaceship

With a 3D wedge shape that tapers in at the front, this spaceship is perfectly aerodynamic. With the help of its slimline wings and tail, it is able to hurtle through space at lightning speed.

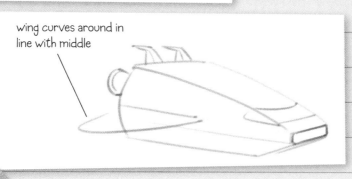

wing curves around in line with middle

wavy fire

shading added

219 Ray gun

Able to vanquish enemies with its super-fast trigger action, this ray gun is futuristic technology at its best. Its heat ray bursts out of the barrel with 100% accuracy.

TIP

Check out Perspective and 3D on page 30 of the introduction to learn more about 3D forms!

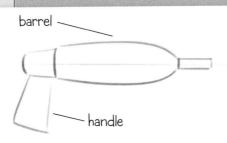

barrel

handle

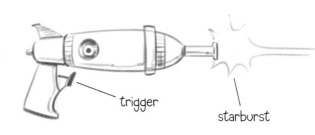

trigger

starburst

220 Enemy spaceship

This ship looks menacing with its insect-like appearance, razor-sharp wings and needle-like tail. Its lightweight structure allows quick moves during battle.

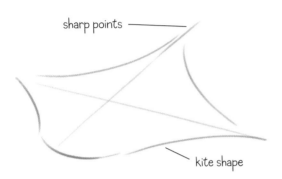

sharp points

kite shape

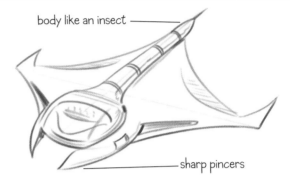

body like an insect

sharp pincers

TIP

Check out Action and Poses on page 10 of the introduction to learn more about basic poses!

221 Cyborg

Half man, half robot, this cyborg is all powerful and intuitive, and wears sleek, ray-gun-proof armour. He is a loyal servant to the crew of mission control and has super-human fighting skills.

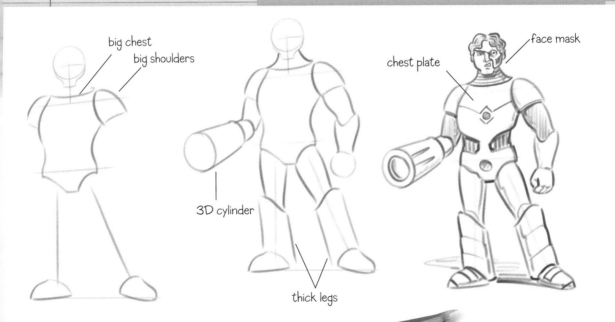

big chest

big shoulders

3D cylinder

chest plate

face mask

thick legs

222 Futuristic motorbike

With a streamlined look and little detail, this motorbike is truly space age. Its sleek and aerodynamic design helps to propel it forwards at the speed of light.

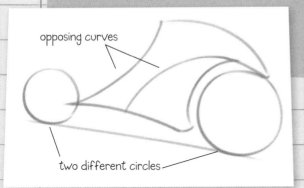

opposing curves

two different circles

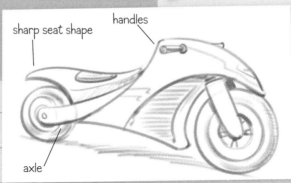

sharp seat shape

handles

axle

Basic robot shapes

You can build robots from basic geometric and irregular shapes. Observe the different shapes that are used for the foundation of each drawing. Each robot is developed from the shapes by adding limbs, mechanical parts and other patterns and details. Try to create some robots using your own chosen shapes. The possibilities are endless!

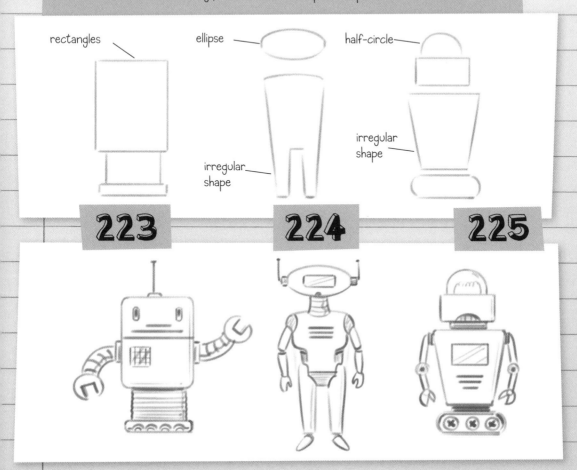

rectangles

ellipse

half-circle

irregular shape

irregular shape

223

224

225

FANTASTIC FAIRIES

Are fairies real or fantasy? Stories of fairy sightings have been part of folklore for generations. These tiny winged creatures are magical beings that live in gardens and forests. They can make rainbows appear in sparkling water. Butterflies and bees are their friends. When summer is over they make the leaves change and during spring they help the flowers bloom. Fairies may watch over Mother Nature, but they can be little tricksters, too!

226 Classic fairy

This dainty little fairy sits happily on her toadstool platform, basking in the forest that surrounds her. Her butterfly-shaped wings highlight her beauty. A caretaker of the forest, this fairy can't wait bring on springtime.

1 Draw the fairy's delicate form. Draw her head and face cross followed by her neck and chest. Add her thin arms then her extended leg. Now draw her bent leg.

2 Draw her wavy hair and the torn edges of her dress's hemline. Draw the top of the dress and add her knees. Darken and define her outline.

3 Draw the fine texture of the fairy's hair then add her headband. Draw the circle pattern on the toadstool. Sketch her facial features over the cross and add her curvy butterfly wings. Add shading and she is ready to make a rainbow appear.

Silly vs. scared

A character can show a variety of emotions. Try drawing your fairy with a silly expression, then with a scared look. When you have finished these pictures, have a go at drawing your fairy showing a completely different emotion of your choice.

227 Silly

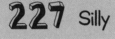

228 Scared

229 Pixie

Test flight in action! This pixie is trying out a new move. She's spinning around and getting a bit dizzy in the process. Pixies are little tricksters so they are always up to funny business.

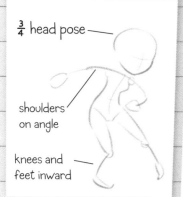

¾ head pose

shoulders on angle

knees and feet inward

hair sticks up

pointy ear

fine wings

frayed edge

movement lines

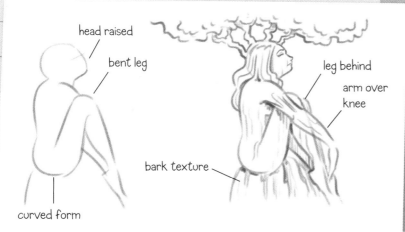

head raised

bent leg

bark texture

curved form

leg behind

arm over knee

230

Dryad

Part of nature, this nymph is a spirit of the forest. She watches over the tree she lives in, protecting it from harm. If a human were to damage the tree, the dryad would punish them. If the tree were to die, she would disappear.

231 Sprite

Sprites are creatures of water, so their natural environment must be cool and peaceful. They are very playful and like to torment butterflies. When summer is over, sprites change the colour of the leaves.

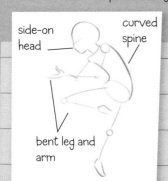

side-on head

curved spine

bent leg and arm

wiggly hair

water droplet

pointy ear

crinkled edge

232 Male elf

Elves have human-like qualities, except for their pointed ears. Male elves are skilful archers with great endurance. Elves also have keen hearing and sight – but they are unable to grow any facial hair!

1 Draw the elf's head (with face cross), pointy collar and chest on an angle. Sketch his thin 'A'-shaped legs. Add the details of his boots.

2 Draw the elf's bent arm across his chest. Add his straight arm pointing up. Draw his hair, shorts and curly boot tips.

3 Draw the elf's face over the cross. Sketch his bow inside his hand and the string pulling back in his other hand. Now add the arrow. Draw the details of his costume with the tails flapping below. Add his arrow pouch. Shade his figure and add the branch and your elf will release the arrow!

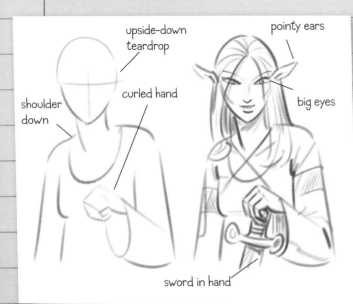

upside-down teardrop

pointy ears

shoulder down

curled hand

big eyes

sword in hand

233

Female elf

Female elves are beautiful and divine creatures with slightly pale skin. They have fragile features and hair that is golden like the sun. Elves have stars in their big eyes and wear delicate and translucent clothing.

234 Gnome

This small earth-dwelling creature lives at the bottom of the garden. He resembles an old man and has a round face and short limbs. His pointed hat and jolly expression are typical of his kind.

pointed hat

rounded face

square shape

jolly expression

short arms

criss-cross pattern

oval chest

small pebble-shaped face

open legs

club in hand

tired expression

hand on knee

235

Troll

A magical creature, the troll lives in caves in the woods. He is a sleepy character who gets easily confused. He has a wispy beard and hair, and his nose is long and round. You may find him looking for a toadstool ring.

Contrasting characters

These two characters couldn't be more different! The gremlin is aggressive and is showing a determined pose, pulling at the cord. The leprechaun is a jovial and energetic character, clicking his heels together.

236 Gremlin

237 Leprechaun

SPOOKY

Spooky, creepy and downright scary – beware of things that go bump in the night! And don't say we didn't warn you about the haunted house. Did you just feel a chill go up your spine? The midnight rattling of chains has begun. You are surely doomed! Check the cupboard for skeletons and make sure you cover your neck, because Dracula is coming your way!

238 Haunted house

The haunted house sits eerily on the hill. Dark and empty, it's just waiting for someone to enter. Locals are always daring each other to venture inside and discover who or what lives there. I wonder what ghostly surprises are creeping around in the hallways?

1 Draw the middle part of the roof, then the outer edges. Add the box shapes for the base of the house.

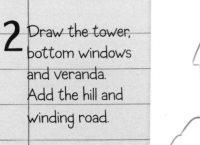

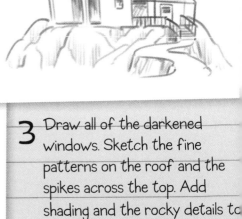

2 Draw the tower, bottom windows and veranda. Add the hill and winding road.

3 Draw all of the darkened windows. Sketch the fine patterns on the roof and the spikes across the top. Add shading and the rocky details to the hill. Draw the banister, moon and bat, and let the fun begin!

Fright night

Here are some typical scary characters that you may find inside a haunted house. Imagine these frightening creatures jumping out at you from behind a door on a dark night. You would jump out of your skin!

239

240

241

head on angle

A-shaped legs

curled collar

cape is moving

242

Dracula

Dracula has woken as day turned into night. He has emerged from his coffin with his cape flapping and his collar sitting upright. That determined look means business. He is ready for his next victim!

3D shape

shadow behind

TIP

Check out Body Language on page 14 of the introduction to learn more about body expression and emotion!

243 Bat

This bat is patrolling the night sky, screeching as he goes. His spiky wings and devilish expression warn you to stay out of his way. He is trying to find a dark, cold place to hang upside-down for a nap.

guideline

face cross

oversized ears

devilish expression

spiky wings

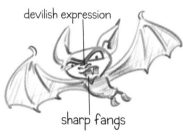

sharp fangs

244 Classic witch

This witch roams the night sky by the light of the moon, cackling as she goes. You wouldn't want to meet her on dark night, with her large nose and chin both covered in warts. She'd frighten the living daylights out of you!

1 Draw the broom on an angle and the witch's curved body perched on top. Add her pointed jaw and hat.

2 Draw her bulbous nose, her hair and her small feet. Sketch both of her arms.

3 Draw her angry eye and brow. Add her open mouth and teeth. Create a line pattern for the broom and her hair. Define her hat and add warts and hair to her face. Define the outline and add shading. Draw the night sky to set the scene.

245 Cauldron

This metal cooking vessel bubbles away over the fire as the witch stirs in her ingredients – dragon's scale, lizard's leg and eye of newt. What a gross concoction!

ellipse

handles

steam

fire

coals

246 Pumpkin

Otherwise known as a jack-o'-lantern, this pumpkin has been carved with an evil expression. Its 3D form is lit from within to highlight its creepy grin.

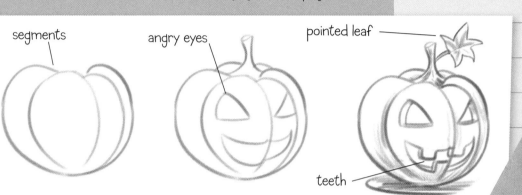

segments

angry eyes

pointed leaf

teeth

247 Black cat

A black cat is seen as a sign of bad luck! It arches its back and fluffs out its tail when it senses that something bad is about to happen. If you're superstitious, walk the other way!

half-circle

arched back

zigzag

legs behind

shadow

shading across

248

Double, double, toil and trouble

This wicked witch is up to no good, concocting an evil spell with all manner of wicked ingredients. Use the drawing skills you have learnt to create a scene. Add other elements that you think will develop the story.

95

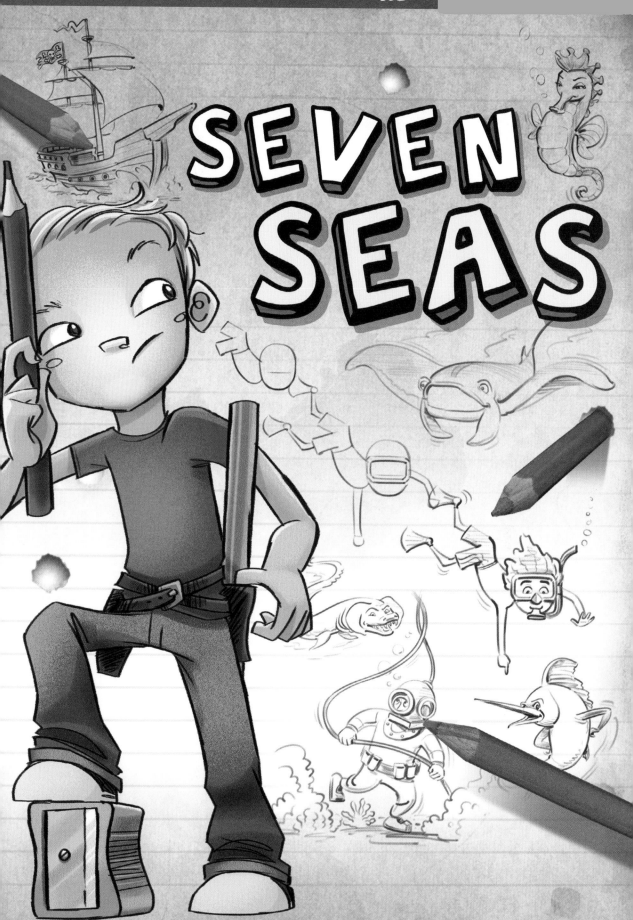

SEA GIANTS

Witnessing the giants of the seven seas is an adventurer's dream. Their sheer size and the unusual manner they exhibit make them a sight to behold. This is why people are drawn to the adventure. Imagine viewing an enormous whale shark bobbing up near the side of your boat, or watching a giant squid curl out its tentacles as you snorkel beneath the sea. You're in the land of the giants!

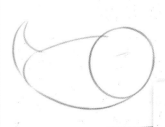

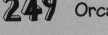

249 Orca

These unusual creatures are found from polar waters to tropical seas. Orcas have a reputation for predatory behaviour, but are very social animals that can be taught special tricks!

1 Draw a round head and a solid body with a curved, pointed tail.

2 Add a pointed dorsal fin and a flipper below. Draw two small leaf shapes for his tail.

3 Lightly draw a patchy pattern on his body. Add a big, open, smiley mouth then define his outline. Draw his eye and tiny teeth. Softly shade his body and sketch the wavy lines around him. Now he's ready to play!

250

Fun and energy!

Add some energy and movement to a drawing by sketching your characters in fun poses. In this drawing, the orcas are having a great time. Their spines have been curved around, their flippers are extended and the water splashing shows their excitement!

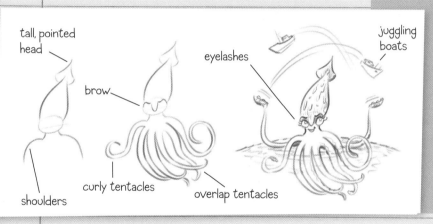

tall, pointed head

brow

eyelashes

juggling boats

shoulders

curly tentacles

overlap tentacles

251
Giant squid

This mysterious beast has the largest eyes in the animal kingdom. She may look innocent enough, but don't let that cute expression fool you. Fishermen fear her because she likes to juggle boats!

252 Manta ray

The manta ray is a gigantic creature who loves to spread his enormous pectoral wings. He sometimes looks like he's flying through the open water. He's a very happy ray!

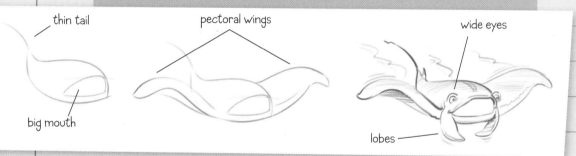

thin tail

pectoral wings

wide eyes

big mouth

lobes

253 Marlin

The marlin is a tough sea giant who's itching to win a fight with any fishing line. His curved spine, angry expression and forward-leaning pose show he means business.

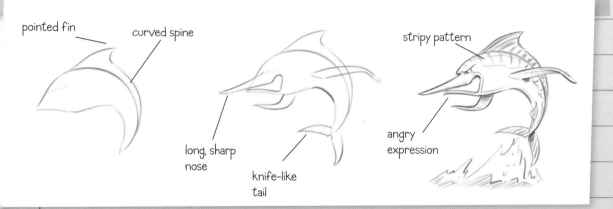

pointed fin

curved spine

stripy pattern

long, sharp nose

angry expression

knife-like tail

254 Polar bear

This polar bear is hanging out in the Arctic Circle, looking mighty cool. He's catching up on some reading and sucking down an iced drink. He may be a powerful predator, but he knows how to relax!

1 Draw the polar bear's body shape with a pointed head. Sketch the ice below him with a flattened circular top.

2 Draw his front arm, then the one behind. Form the edges of the ice. Add his ear and curved legs.

3 Draw the polar bear's glasses and his peaked hat, then sketch his mouth and nose. Draw his fingers and toes. Add his open book and his drink. Create his furry outline and add soft shading. What a cool bear!

255 Sperm whale

The biggest whale of the ocean has found a little friend to frolic with. This whale has a large curved body with a tail that tapers out. He's having fun bouncing his fish friend on top of his spout!

curved body

tail tapers out

wavy waterline

water spout

leaf-like tail

flat on bottom

These three species of shark each have different body shapes. Observe the three individual shapes. The whale shark is a teardrop shape, the hammerhead has a wedge on top of its curved body and the sand tiger shark has an angular body with a turned-up nose.

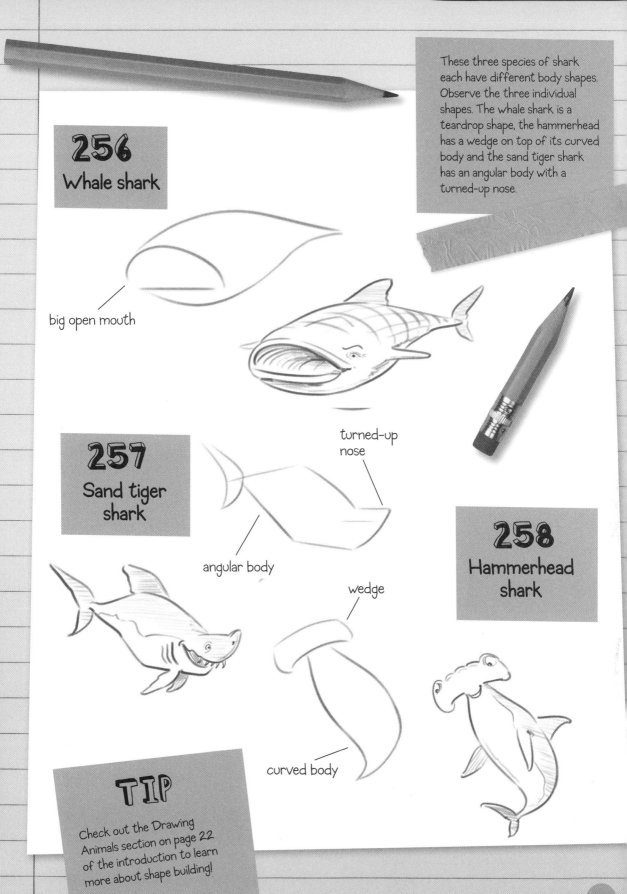

256
Whale shark

big open mouth

257
Sand tiger shark

turned-up nose

angular body

258
Hammerhead shark

wedge

curved body

TIP

Check out the Drawing Animals section on page 22 of the introduction to learn more about shape building!

OCEAN CREATURES

Many curious creatures can be found swimming around in the ocean. Their striking details create a wondrous display of moving pictures. Think of the spiky blowfish that puffs up when in danger, or the stripy angelfish with its pointy profile and pouting lips. And what's that glowing over there with long, wavy tentacles? It's a jellyfish, of course!

259 Dolphin

These friendly creatures are very playful. People are drawn to them because of their great intelligence. Some people even believe dolphins have natural healing powers!

1 Draw the dolphin's curved body with a snout and a fan-shaped tail.

2 Draw her dorsal fin and fins either side of her chest. Add eyes above her snout.

3 Draw the dolphin's smile, and her eyelashes and pupils. Define the dolphin's outline, then add a light level of shading to shape her form.

260

Humanising animals

We're used to seeing dolphins in the sea. Instead, why not draw your dolphins chatting at a party, having a good time? You can humanise animals by putting them in an unexpected setting and giving them a human pose.

261 Angelfish

This diamond-shaped fish is an angel of the ocean. He loves serenading his friends with an angelic tune on his harp. His long head, fin and snout define his unique character.

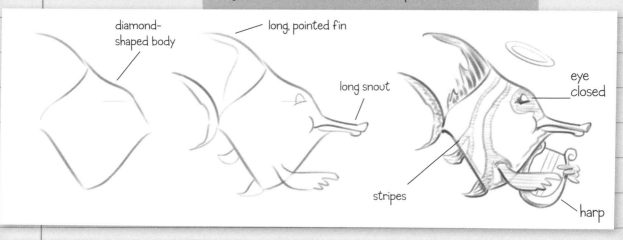

diamond-shaped body

long, pointed fin

long snout

eye closed

stripes

harp

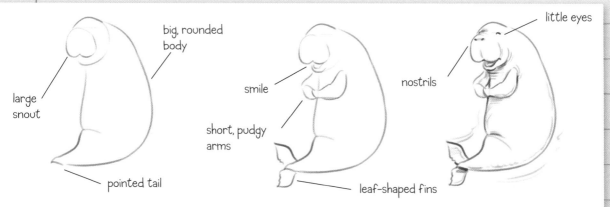

big, rounded body

little eyes

large snout

smile

nostrils

short, pudgy arms

pointed tail

leaf-shaped fins

262 Walrus

Slow and a little bit goofy, this roly-poly walrus likes to laze around in the ocean. He has a big, rotund body and a round snout, and he's laughing, too!

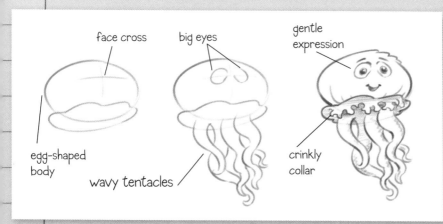

face cross

big eyes

gentle expression

egg-shaped body

wavy tentacles

crinkly collar

263

Jellyfish

This happy little jellyfish propels himself through the water with his thick tentacles. His crinkly collar and gentle expression make him look innocent.

Blowfish

This blowfish can inflate like a piece of bubblegum, growing from a teardrop shape to a big, round bubble. This drawing is done in two separate stages. Study the changes between each step before you begin.

264 Deflated blowfish

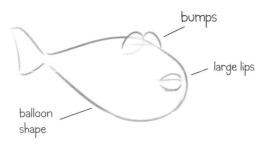

bumps

large lips

balloon shape

surprised expression

spiky outline

265 Inflated blowfish

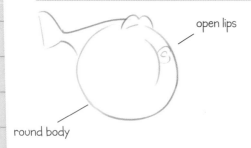

open lips

round body

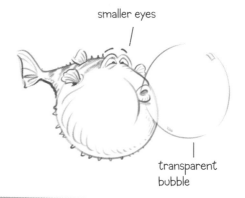

smaller eyes

transparent bubble

266 Flying fish

It's a bird! It's a plane! No, it's a flying fish! This freaky fish's fins are like a bird's wings. Look how it launches itself out of the water.

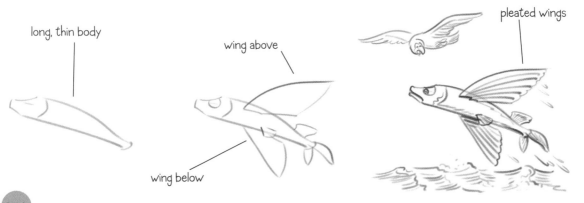

long, thin body

wing above

pleated wings

wing below

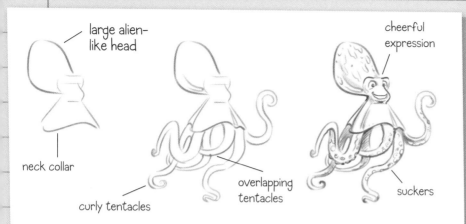

large alien-like head

neck collar

curly tentacles

overlapping tentacles

cheerful expression

suckers

267

Octopus

This cheerful octopus's long tentacles curl and extend as he dances through the ocean! He has an alien-like head and a collar for a neck. He also has suckers running down his legs.

268 Clam

This clam is scared of anything that moves across the ocean floor. He'd rather stay in his crinkly-edged shell, only peeking out once in a while!

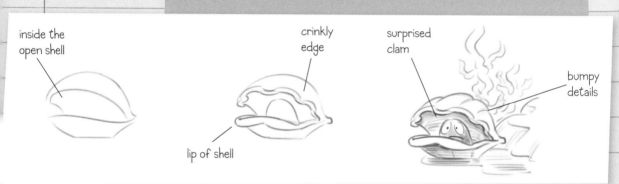

inside the open shell

crinkly edge

surprised clam

bumpy details

lip of shell

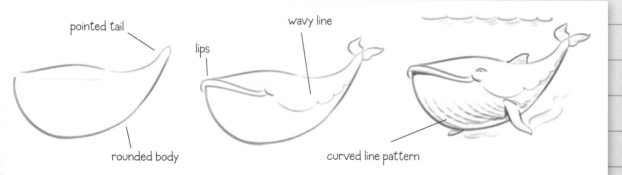

pointed tail

lips

wavy line

rounded body

curved line pattern

269 Blue whale

Life is sweet for this whale! She's happy frolicking in the ocean, propelling her huge body through the water. She's free to do her own thing without a care in the world!

PIRATE ISLAND

Pirates are the most feared sailors of the seven seas. They search for treasure and will take it by any means possible. Hoisted high on their ship is a black flag with a white skull and crossbones. Threatening in appearance and handy with weapons, pirates are not to be messed with. Look out! Hide your treasure maps and your pretty dames; the pirate ship is almost upon us.

270 Blackbeard

The most feared pirate of the seven seas, Blackbeard wants to steal treasure! He uses his terrible reputation and appearance to frighten other sailors and is ready to do battle with those who stand in his way!

1 Draw Blackbeard's skeleton. Draw his head (with a face cross), shoulders, chest, then legs. Sketch his feet against an angled baseline.

2 Build his form around the skeleton. Draw his hat, face and beard. Follow with his thick arm shapes and his sword. Define his clothing and legs.

3 Define his facial features, beard and hand. Draw his sashes, belt and pistols. Add detail to his clothing, sword and shoes then add shading to his whole figure. Arrr, me hearties!

Facial hair

Whether it's a full beard, a sophisticated moustache or curly mutton chops, try mixing it up by giving your pirate different facial hair. This gives your subject more character. These three pirates are certainly hairy!

271

272

273

face cross

floppy hair

curved spine

skeleton

base of sword

puffy sleeves

bare stomach

coin belt

274 Pirate girl

Arrr! Take that! This pirate girl is nifty with a sword and is happy to challenge anyone who'll take her on. She is a no-nonsense buccaneer who is ready for anything!

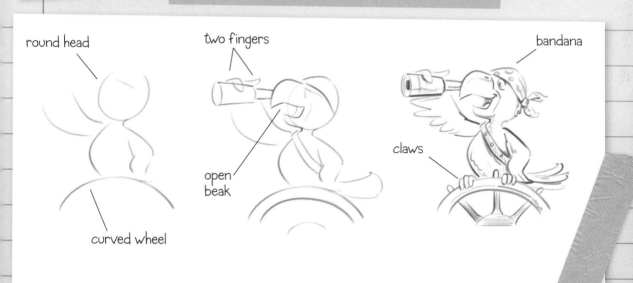

round head

two fingers

bandana

open beak

claws

curved wheel

275 Parrot

Where would a pirate be without his trusty sidekick, the parrot? This parrot is always on the lookout for ships approaching, or watching for land in the distance. He's handy with the spyglass and doesn't mind taking the wheel!

Motley crew

Look out for this motley crew – they mean business! They're mad, bad and out to steal your treasure. These pirates come in all shapes and sizes – thin, fat and short. Study their sizes in relation to each other, especially in the first stage of drawing.

276

face cross

thin

277

big and round

278

short and stumpy

When drawing your motley crew, start with the basic shapes. Note that all the crew are drawn in front-on poses. Draw their head shapes first, followed by their chest and legs. Their outlines are drawn around the shapes.

craggy face

large features

puffy hair

sash

jagged sword

big hands

279 Treasure chest

Riches aplenty! These jewels and gold sparkle in the light. The wooden box itself is a three-dimensional shape seen on an angle. Imagine finding this buried treasure!

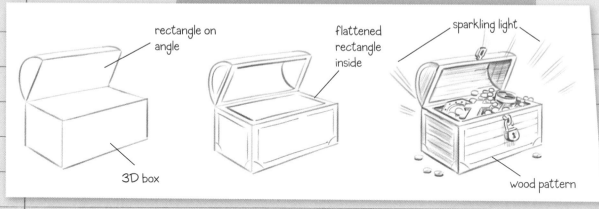

rectangle on angle

flattened rectangle inside

sparkling light

3D box

wood pattern

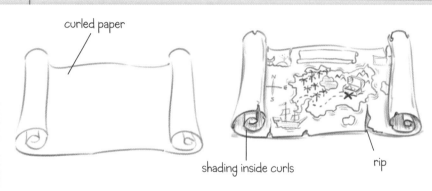

curled paper

shading inside curls

rip

280

Treasure map

'X' marks the spot. A pirate's mission is to find buried treasure. Roll open the map to reveal how many steps forward you need to take – then start digging!

281 Pirate ship

A menacing ship emerges from the fog, ready for battle! With its skull-and-crossbones flag, billowing sails and portholes below, this is a classic pirate ship.

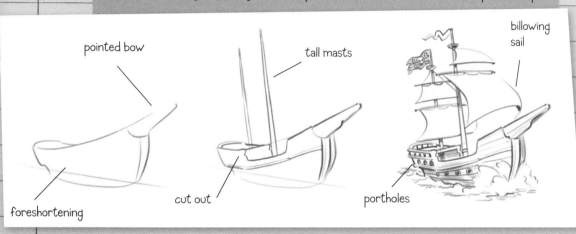

pointed bow

tall masts

billowing sail

foreshortening

cut out

portholes

DEEP-SEA DIVE

There are some truly creepy creatures in the darkest depths of the ocean. The deeper you dive, the weirder the marine life becomes. It's like you're in a science fiction movie. See that anglerfish, with its dorsal spine dangling a light in front of it? There's a blob fish, too! It looks like a mass of jelly. Oh, and don't forget the elongated frill shark. It looks like it's from prehistoric times!

282

Deep-sea diver with frill shark

Diving to the bottom of the deep ocean requires a special suit and breathing equipment. It is very dark down there, so the creatures that live there haven't seen much light. They're quite freaky to look at!

1 Draw a round head with a curvy body on an angle, with one leg lifted off the ground.

2 Draw the helmet with two circular windows. Draw curved bands around the neck and waist.

3 Draw fingers inside the hand shapes. Add detail to the helmet and shoes. Draw 3D boxes for weights around his belt.

4 Draw the diver's face looking up through one of the windows. Add rivets around the neck, and the wavy oxygen line coming from the helmet. Draw the rope he's holding, then add further details and shading to his suit. Now draw the wavy sea plants and movement lines, then challenge yourself by drawing the frill shark (see page 111) above him.

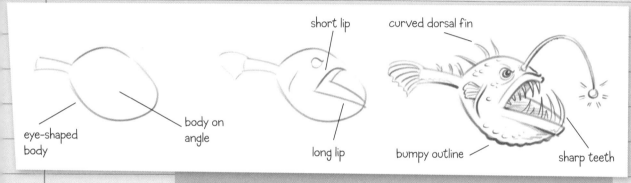

short lip

curved dorsal fin

eye-shaped body

body on angle

long lip

bumpy outline

sharp teeth

283 Anglerfish

You won't miss this creepy fish in the darkest depths of the ocean! His spiky fins and razor-sharp teeth make a real statement, while his curved dorsal fin lights his way.

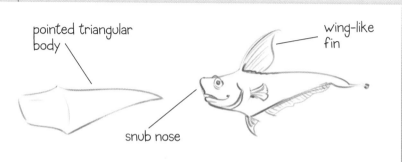

pointed triangular body

wing-like fin

snub nose

284 Ratfish

This strange creature has a triangular, elongated body. He has a snub nose and a big, wing-like fin. He may look harmless at first, but you won't think that when he uses his body to crush his prey!

285 Blob fish

This fish looks just like a big blob of jelly, and he doesn't have much energy to propel himself around! He has a large, droopy nose and a sad frown on his face.

pebble-shaped body

large, droopy nose

curved fins

286 Frill shark

This fish looks prehistoric! Sailors have mistaken him for a sea serpent or the Loch Ness Monster. He has a long, curly tail and frilly details over his body.

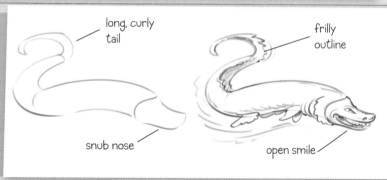

long, curly tail

frilly outline

snub nose

open smile

LIFE'S A BEACH

Sun, sea and surf! The mere scent of the sea air promises a fun day at the beach. The sound of waves crashing against the sand and the sight of the sparkling blue water are bound to put a smile on your face. Jump on a surfboard or cast a line and see what's biting. Play on the golden sand and watch the happy crabs crawling into their burrows. Whatever you do, relax and take it easy – life's a beach!

287 Surfer Girl

Catching an epic wave is a huge thrill! Ripping through the foamy surf on your surfboard and seeing how long you can stay on is an awesome challenge. Gnarly dude!

1 Draw the surfer's skeleton. Sketch a round head, face cross and spine. Draw the body shape then add the joints and lines for her arms and legs. Draw her feet on an angle.

2 Build the form of her body around the skeleton.

3 Draw her fingers inside the hand shapes. Draw her facial features and wavy hair. Define the details of her wetsuit and draw a surfboard beneath her feet. Now sketch the wavy and puffy lines for the water. Hang five, surfer girl!

288

Action!

When drawing someone in action, consider the type of pose you are trying to achieve. The best approach is to draw a skeleton first. The angle of the spine and the positioning of the head and limbs determine the pose. Have a go at drawing these two using the process above.

289

pie-shaped body

wide eyes

bent claw

claw sits forward

happy mouth

pincers

290
Happy crab

This crab is a happy chap! He has wide, alert eyes and an open mouth with his tongue hanging out. The bumpy texture on his shell makes it look hard. He's ready to chomp down on that ice-cream!

pie-shaped body

claw points up

sad eyes close together

bent claw

dripping ice-cream

wobbly mouth

291
Sad crab

How things have changed! The hot sun has ruined the crab's day. His eyes are turned inward and his mouth is wobbly. His ice-cream has dripped everywhere. Oh dear!

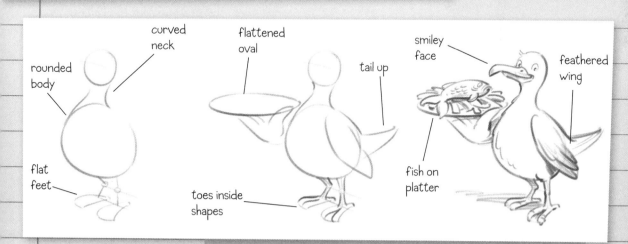

curved neck

flattened oval

smiley face

feathered wing

rounded body

tail up

flat feet

toes inside shapes

fish on platter

292 Hungry seagull

This little scavenger has certainly been busy! Look at the feast he's found for dinner. He's very proud of himself, and can't wait gobble up his meal.

293 Lifeguard

Policing the beach is a lifeguard's job. They make sure people swim between the flags so they are in the safest place. A lifeguard rescues people when they get into trouble and administers first aid. Where would we be without them?

1 Draw the lifeguard's curved torso and straight shoulders, then add his shorts.

2 Draw his angular head and the face cross. Sketch his arms and his open legs, with his feet on an angle.

3 Draw his face over the cross. Add his chest details and draw the board in his hand. Sketch his cap and shade his shorts. Define his outline and draw the beach scene behind. Anyone need rescuing?

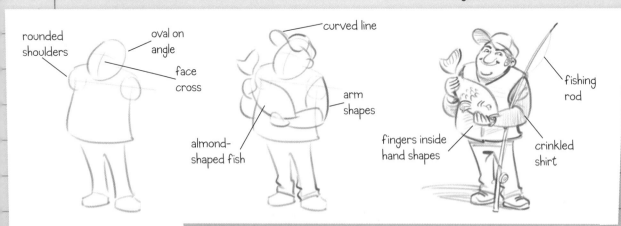

rounded shoulders

oval on angle

face cross

curved line

almond-shaped fish

arm shapes

fingers inside hand shapes

fishing rod

crinkled shirt

294 Fisherman

This jolly fisherman is very pleased with his catch of the day. He's holding his big fish on an angle, with his rod tucked inside his elbow. Fish and chips for dinner tonight!

Beach family

This happy family are headed for a relaxing day at the seaside. From tall to short and big to small, they are all different. They are determined to get a good position on the beach.

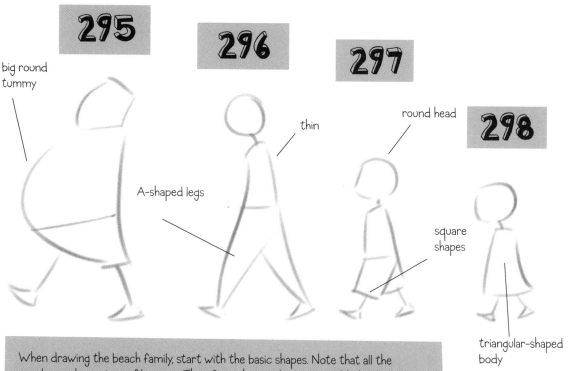

295

big round tummy

296

thin

297

round head

A-shaped legs

298

square shapes

triangular-shaped body

When drawing the beach family, start with the basic shapes. Note that all the people are drawn in profile poses. Their faces, hair and arms are added, followed by the things they are carrying. Their outlines are drawn around the shapes.

TIP

Check out the Body Language section on page 14 of the introduction to learn more about body shapes!

OCEAN SPORTS

If its action you're after, try some ocean adventure. Kite surfing lifts you off the water so you can fly like a bird. Scuba diving takes you to the ocean floor to view the marine life below the surface. What about speeding around on a jet ski? It's pretty cool zipping across the water with the wind in your hair! Ocean sports make for an exciting pastime for young and old.

299 Jet ski

Zipping along at high speed, jumping out of the water and listening to the roar of the engine: jet skis are fun to ride! They are a thrill-seeker's dream, but make sure you're riding safely!

1 Draw the boy's round head, face cross and rectangular body on an angle. Draw the curved outline of the jet ski underneath.

2 Sketch the T-shaped handles of the jet ski. Add the boy's arms, and leg and add a line to show the seat.

3 Draw his face over the cross then sketch his floppy hair. Add his fingers and draw his striped top. Draw any extra details for the jet ski, then add the splashing water. Off he goes!

More fun!

The boy looks like he's having a great time zipping through the water. Observe the angle of the jet ski. Draw that first, then sketch the boy on top. Make sure you get the angle of his spine correct!

300

301

left arm and right leg forward

paddle on an angle

jumping dolphin

right arm and left leg back

longboard

302
Paddleboarder

Standing up on her board, the girl paddles through the water. It's hard to stay upright when the waves roll in and a dolphin is jumping around you! She has to really concentrate.

kayak on angle

paddle across chest

long eye-shape

303 Kayaker

This man is cruising along at a steady pace, pushing through the water. He has to keep a balanced rhythm with his paddle so he won't roll over and get dunked!

Out of the blue

Oh no! I bet he didn't see that coming! This kayaker is a bit stuck. If only his friends could see him now – they wouldn't be able to stop laughing!

304

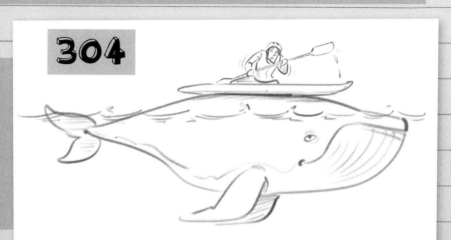

305 Windsurfer

Why is it called a windsurfer? It combines all the elements of sailing and surfing: the wind helps propel it through the water and the rider steers with the sail to manoeuvre the board.

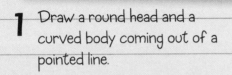

1 Draw a round head and a curved body coming out of a pointed line.

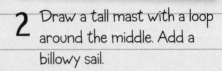

2 Draw a tall mast with a loop around the middle. Add a billowy sail.

3 Draw the windsurfer's front arm, then the one behind holding onto the loop. Draw her big glasses, lips and wavy hair. Define the sailboard and the windsurfer's clothing. Draw a splash of wavy water and add some light shading. Now off she goes!

306

Action and movement

Try drawing your windsurfer in two new poses. Get into the action by drawing her on a sharp angle. Also try sketching her lifting her sailboard off the water. Pay attention to the angle of the sailboard and her spine.

307

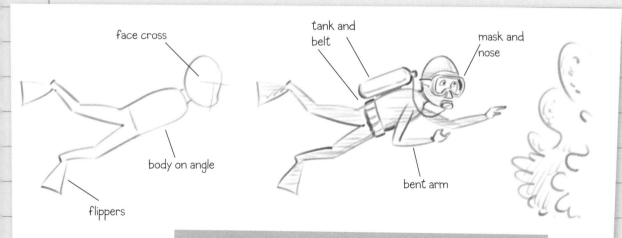

face cross

tank and belt

mask and nose

body on angle

bent arm

flippers

308 Scuba diving

Down in the depths of the ocean, this scuba diver is ready for a marine adventure. Goggles, an oxygen tank, a wet suit and flippers help him swim through the deep water. He looks like he's floating on air.

face cross

face over cross

on an angle

feet inside

309 Kite surfer

This kite surfer is showing off to his audience on the beach. He's confident in his special tricks – surfing, jumping and flips.

TIP

Check out the Action and Poses section on page 10 of the introduction to learn more about soft and dynamic movement!

SHIPS AHOY!

Ahoy, seafaring folk! Come and join us on a journey across the oceans. You'll see a super-sized luxury ocean liner that travels around the world, and a speedboat that likes to zip across the waters. The sleek, athletic yacht is always vying for our attention, sailing to exotic locations. Then there's the hard-working ferry that likes sightseeing in picturesque ports. Jump aboard. It's time for an awesome trip!

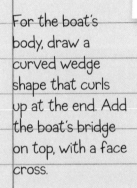

310 Tugboat

This handy little boat helps around the harbour, day and night. He moves vessels that can't move themselves, using his power to tug them out of the way. He's so happy as he cruises the waters! Toot!

1 For the boat's body, draw a curved wedge shape that curls up at the end. Add the boat's bridge on top, with a face cross.

2 Draw a curved line under the bow. Add a small rectangular shape to the bridge. Draw his curved cap and viewing window.

3 Draw four portholes, from small to big. Add a big smile across the bow and eyes inside the window. Add the tall smoke stack with a life buoy below, and draw the light on his cap. Define and shade any further details. Now draw puffs of smoke and water below. Toot, toot!

311

Different expressions

Now that you know how to draw the little tugboat, try giving him a determined look, chugging hard and tugging a ship. Then draw him looking worried.

WORRIED

312

DETERMINED

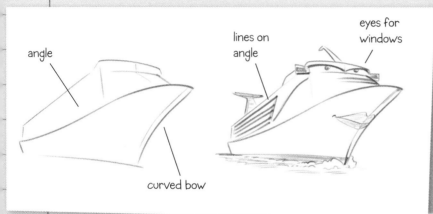

angle

lines on angle

eyes for windows

curved bow

313
Ocean liner

'Luxury' is the best word to describe this big liner. She shows off her many levels, enormous bridge and streamlined appearance as she travels around the world.

314   Yacht

This boat is a real beauty that loves sailing around islands in crystal blue waters. Her billowing sails and pointed bow give her a sophisticated look. She loves anchoring at sunset to watch the spectacular view.

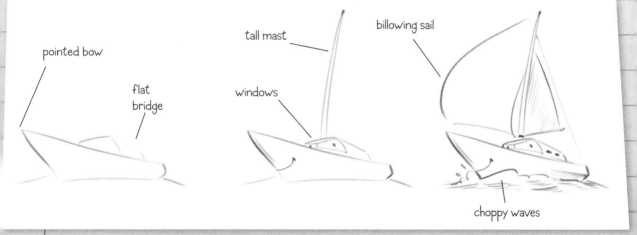

pointed bow

flat bridge

tall mast

billowing sail

windows

choppy waves

315   Fishing boat

This fishing boat is an old seafarer – a creaky boat that's been on the sea for years. He's an experienced traveller with a tough exterior that's been worn away by the salt and water.

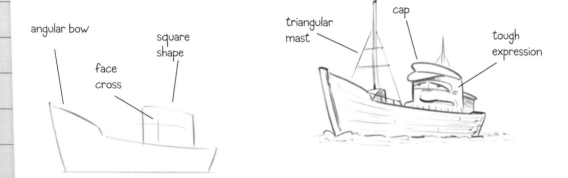

angular bow

face cross

square shape

triangular mast

cap

tough expression

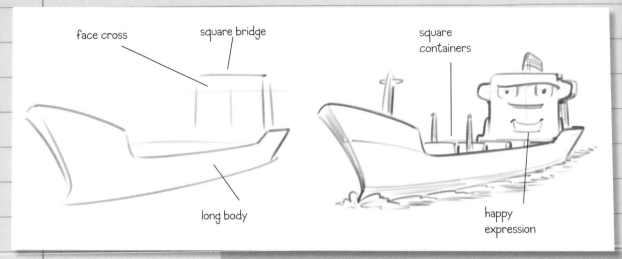

face cross · square bridge · square containers · long body · happy expression

316 Cargo boat

This boat is happy chugging along from one country to another, importing and exporting goods. He takes care of his load, trying to avoid reefs and rough seas where he can.

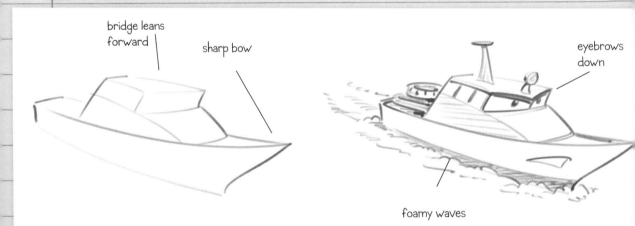

bridge leans forward · sharp bow · eyebrows down · foamy waves

317 Police boat

Here's a young, strong and fast boat that's always on the lookout for trouble. He's out to catch the bad guys at any cost! His serious look and sharp angles display his determination to succeed.

TIP

Check out the Perspective and 3D section on page 30 of the introduction to learn more about 3D shapes!

318 Speedboat

Speedy by name and speedy by nature, this thrillseeker is happiest when he's driving fast. He likes to speed around buoys and leap out of the water. He's bigger at the front and thinner at the back, which helps him go fast!

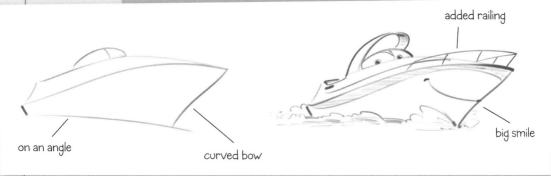

added railing

on an angle

curved bow

big smile

319 Speedboat race

The shapes on the left are sharp and angular, which makes them look fast, as though they're lurching forward. A more rounded shape would not give the drawing the same look or feel.

CORAL REEF

Under the sea, there's a rainbow-coloured paradise just waiting to be explored. Snorkel below the water's surface and discover an array of amazing creatures in a myriad of shapes and patterns. Join the clownfish, parrotfish, seahorse and swordfish, and immerse yourself in their constant activity. There's entertainment and delight to be found in these sparkling blue waters!

320 Sea turtle

Sea turtles live in the ocean most of the time, gliding through water. The female travels huge distances to lay her eggs, which are shaped like ping-pong balls. She pulls herself onto the sand with her flippers to dig a nest where she lays the eggs and then covers them over.

1 Draw a rock shape for the turtle's body. Add its neck and a pointed head.

2 Draw flippers either side of the body and two more at the end of his shell. Outline his wrinkly neck and draw a smiley mouth.

3 Draw a bumpy pattern on his skin and a brick-like pattern on his shell. Define the turtle's outline and draw his eye and nostril. Draw wavy lines for the water. Now your turtle can catch the slipstream!

321

Split personalities

A character's age can be determined by changing just a few details.

Drawing a hunched back, a frown, wrinkles and a walking stick can show an older personality.

322

Drawing an alert look, a perky pose and a music player can depict a youthful personality.

323 Parrot fish

Parrot fish may not be able to fly like their namesakes, but they are just as colourful. Parrot fish always have a slightly surprised look. The decorative patterns on their body highlight their beauty.

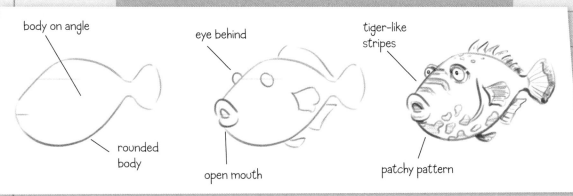

body on angle

eye behind

tiger-like stripes

rounded body

open mouth

patchy pattern

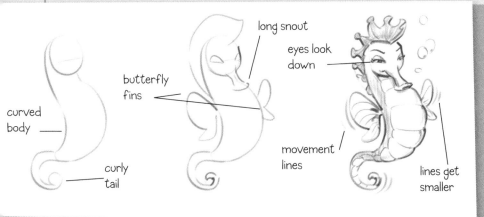

curved body

butterfly fins

curly tail

long snout

eyes look down

movement lines

lines get smaller

324

Seahorse

This creature's horse-like features are obvious. His mane and long snout make him stand out from the crowd. His butterfly wings and curly tail are real showstoppers.

325 Starfish

Just like the stars in the sky, this cute sea creature has five points. This little guy is happy lazing around on the ocean floor, waiting to be admired by people who snorkel by!

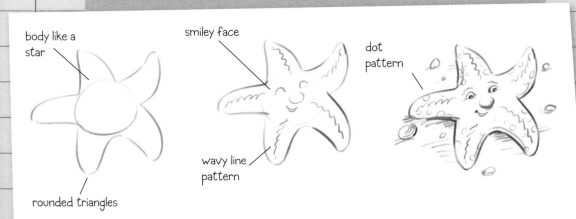

body like a star

smiley face

dot pattern

wavy line pattern

rounded triangles

wavy fin

stripe pattern

egg-shaped face

front fins moving

happy expression

326 Clownfish

This fish loves to clown around. He's happy flitting in and out of his anemone all day long! His striking details and patterns aren't just for fun, though. They help him to be clearly distinguished from other fish species.

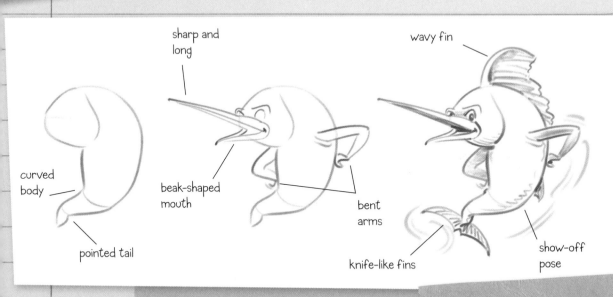

sharp and long

wavy fin

curved body

beak-shaped mouth

bent arms

pointed tail

knife-like fins

show-off pose

327 Swordfish

This swordfish is pretty proud of himself. Can't you tell from the way he's posing? If you had a sword for a mouth, you'd think you were pretty cool, too. His knife-like fins show that he's not to be messed with!

126

328 Snorkeller

This snorkeller is having a wonderful time swimming through the warm ocean water. He is marvelling at the scene of colourful fishes and coral below him, pointing at the amazing discoveries he's made!

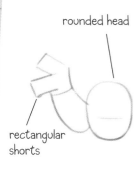

rounded head

rectangular shorts

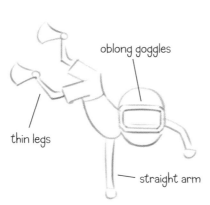

oblong goggles

thin legs

straight arm

wavy hair

looking down

open flat hand

329

Create a scene

Use some of your characters to create an underwater scene. As your swimmer snorkels by, he almost collides with a surprised parrot fish. Below, a happy clownfish pokes his head out from his anemone, and a starfish looks up from the ocean floor.

TIME WARP

BEFORE TIME

Dinosaurs roamed the Earth around 250 million years ago, during the Mesozoic era. Different dinosaur species lived during different periods, known as the Cretaceous, Jurassic and Triassic periods. Human beings are relatively new inhabitants of this planet. Imagine if the giant dinosaurs of the past roamed the Earth today! What a sight that would be!

330 Tyrannosaurus rex

Stomp, stomp, stomp! T-rex is making an awful racket. With his massive skull, sharp, fearsome teeth and powerful legs and tail, nothing would stand a chance against this beast!

1 Draw T-rex's block-like head. Add his pebble-shaped body under his chin, on an angle. Connect his neck then add his thighs.

2 Add his thick, curved tail. Draw his straight front leg with an angled foot, then his raised foot. Add his small, curled arms.

3 Draw pointed scales down his back and sharp claws on his feet. Draw his fingers and a big, open mouth. Add his sharp teeth, nostrils and angry eyes. Darken his outline and add a line pattern to his skin. Now just add shading – your T-rex is ready to rumble!

Flipside

T-rex isn't bad all of the time. In the safety of his forest home, his other side really comes out! Here he is having a snooze and being playful!

331

332

TIP

Check out Action and Poses on page 10 of the introduction to learn more about animals in action!

333

Scared velociraptor

What's he running from? I thought *he* was supposed to be the scary one! Velociraptors were deadly carnivores, but this one looks like he's seen a ghost!

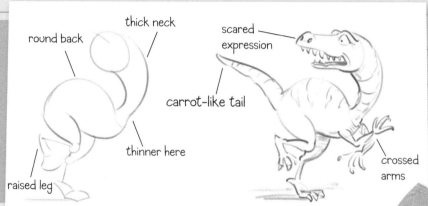

round back

thick neck

scared expression

carrot-like tail

thinner here

raised leg

crossed arms

334 Stegosaurus

This content-looking dinosaur is actually the size of a bus! He's showing off the large, leaf-like plates that run down his back. His tail looks a bit like a spiky plant. Don't be scared – he has a brain the size of a walnut!

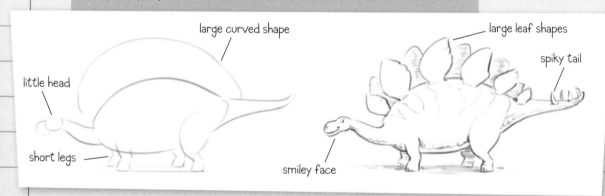

large curved shape

large leaf shapes

spiky tail

little head

short legs

smiley face

335 Plesiosaurus

This marine reptile has a face and fins like a turtle. He looks a little bored. Perhaps he'd be happier walking with the dinosaurs, rather than swimming in circles in the ocean all day!

wavy body shape

ribbed pattern

looking down

rock-shaped head

336 Apatosaurus

Once known as the 'Brontosaurus', this enormous herbivore could grow to around 21 metres (69 feet) long. His long, craning neck is helping him make a meal out of those trees. Check out his whip-like tail!

1 Draw his rounded body then add his long neck and small oval head. Draw the top of his thick tail.

2 Define his head shape and add his open mouth. Draw his thick front legs that are flat on the bottom. Add the shorter legs behind, and his long tail.

3 Add his eye, nostril and the leaves in his mouth. Draw his toes and the crinkles down his neck, then define his outline. Add shading and the ferns behind. Apatosaurus is on the move!

bent neck

knife-like wings

337 Pterodactyl

This flying reptile is on the lookout for his next meal, shrieking as he goes. His giant wings help him soar through the sky, spotting prey, which he will gobble up with his large beak.

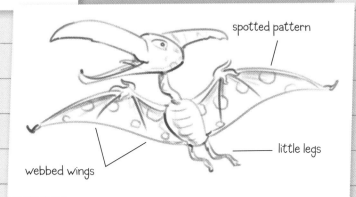

spotted pattern

webbed wings

little legs

338 Triceratops

This horned dinosaur may look like a rhinoceros, but he certainly isn't going to charge at you. He's a happy, bounding Triceratops, full of energy.

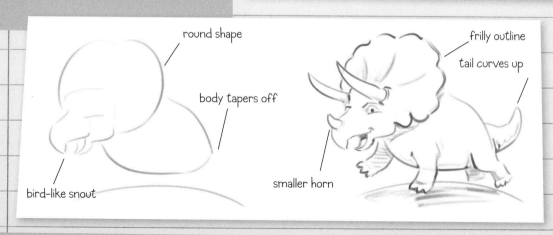

round shape

frilly outline

tail curves up

body tapers off

bird-like snout

smaller horn

From different angles

When the Triceratops is viewed from different perspectives, the shapes used for his head and horns take on a different look. Observe the changes between three-quarter (above), side-on and front-on poses (below). Also note the change in his expression.

TIP

Check out Facial Expressions on page 6 of the introduction to learn more about animal expressions!

339

340

EGYPTOLOGY

Ancient Egypt was a prosperous civilisation based along the River Nile. Ruled by Pharaohs, the ancient Egyptians' achievements were monumental. The pyramids and the Great Sphinx are just two examples of their legacy. Can you imagine trying to build those structures?

341 Pharaoh

The pharaoh was the most powerful person in Ancient Egypt. He made all the laws, owned all the land and collected all the taxes. Ancient Egyptians thought that he represented their gods on here on Earth. No wonder he is such a happy chappie!

1 Draw the Pharaoh's skeleton on an angle, using the guidelines to direct you. Start at the head and work down. Don't forget the face cross.

2 Draw his headpiece and define his face shape. Draw his muscular form around the skeleton.

3 Draw his happy face over the cross. Define his chest and arms then add his staff and hands. Draw his decorative sash then add his feet. Add a slight level of shading over his whole body and draw in the pattern on his headgear and sash. Strike a pose, Pharaoh!

Ancient transport

When drawing ancient transport, you don't have to show it in great detail. It can be conveyed using a few simple shapes and lines. Have a go at drawing this chariot and boat.

342

343

344 Tutankhamen

Otherwise known as King Tut, Tutankhamen inherited the throne at a very young age and died soon after – no one is sure what from. His decorative death mask is much admired.

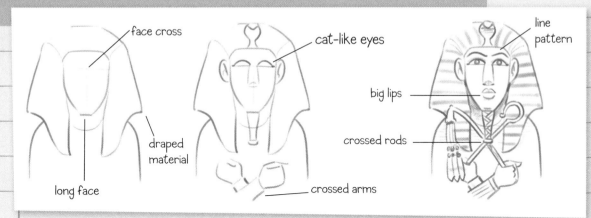

face cross

cat-like eyes

line pattern

big lips

draped material

crossed rods

long face

crossed arms

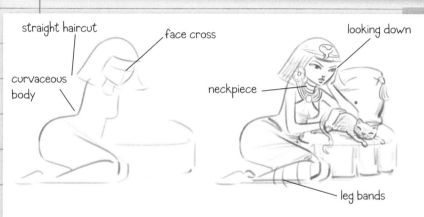

straight haircut

face cross

looking down

curvaceous body

neckpiece

leg bands

345

Cleopatra

Possibly the most famous monarch in world history, Cleopatra was said to be extremely beautiful and intelligent. She looks pretty lonely for someone with the world at her feet!

346 Nefertiti

Much-admired for her elegant beauty, Queen Nefertiti was also strong and considered to be an equal to her husband, King Akhenaten. She was slender and wore a Pharaoh's crown.

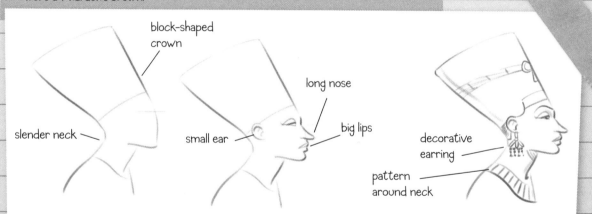

block-shaped crown

long nose

big lips

slender neck

small ear

decorative earring

pattern around neck

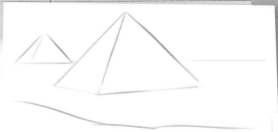

347 Pyramids

One of the Seven Wonders of the Ancient World, the pyramids of Giza are a human triumph. They are an architectural feat, built by 100 000 slaves over 20 years!

1 Draw the large three-dimensional pyramid shape in the foreground, then the smaller one in the distance. Draw the outline of the sand.

2 Draw a fine line pattern on the front of the pyramids and bumpy outlines for the sand around the base. Sketch two palm trees in the front of the picture. Define the outline of the sand and lightly add shading. Your pyramids are ready to be admired!

348 Horus

This is a statue of the falcon god, who was seen as the lord of the sky and represented great cosmic powers. His right eye was the sun and his left eye the moon.

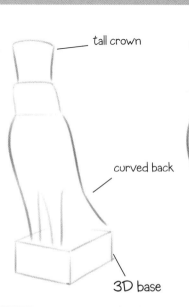

tall crown

curved back

3D base

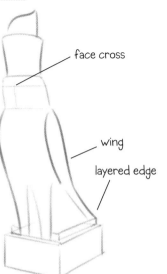

face cross

wing

layered edge

serious expression

tiny chair

349 Temple carvings

You can change your style of drawing to suit the purpose. These three Egyptian gods are worshipped for their control of the elements. To make them look like temple carvings, use dark, smooth and clean outlines. They have larger torsos and smaller bodies.

Ra, god of the sun   Set, god of storms   Nut, goddess of the sky

guidelines on angle

looking up

3D base

350 The Great Sphinx

The Great Sphinx is situated near the pyramids of Giza. It has the head of a human and the body of a lion. This huge monument is made of sandstone and is 70 metres (230 feet) long and 20 metres (65 feet) tall.

line pattern

bumpy claws

TIP

Refer to Perspective and 3D on page 30 of the introduction to learn about the fundamentals of perspective!

ANCIENT ROME

The Roman Empire was one of the largest empires of the ancient world. It was an all-powerful civilisation whose army conquered parts of Europe, Asia and Africa. Roman society was structured around religion, particularly their belief in gods like Jupiter, Neptune and Atlas. They believed that the gods were present during important occasions and would be angry if the wrong decisions were made.

351 Caesar

Hail Caesar! Julius Caesar was the leader of the Roman Republic, which he transformed into a huge empire as its dictator. He was a writer of Latin texts, many about his military campaigns and life. He looks pretty serious and pompous in this pose!

1 Draw Caesar's round head and sharp jaw. Add his thick neck and curved body shape.

2 Draw his sharp nose and bent arms. Define his shoulders and draw a sash across his chest. Add his feet.

3 Draw his eye and his frown, making him look pompous. Define his chin and add his hairstyle. Add hand shapes and the folds of his clothing. Now watch him rule his empire!

352 Centurion

353 Civilian in toga

TIP

Check out Designing a Character on page 26 of the introduction to learn about developing your character's personality!

Step back in time

It's all about the costumes with these two. You can show that someone is from a particular era by the clothing that they wear. Details and decoration define your character's personality and can represent the time and place that they come from.

354 Jupiter

Don't make Jupiter angry or he'll show his displeasure by throwing lightning bolts and wreaking havoc from the sky above. His big chest is puffed out and his muscly arm is raised, ready to strike.

large shoulders

puffy hair and beard

toga across chest

big chest

curved back

hand on hip

355 Neptune

Jupiter's brother Neptune is the god of the sea and of horses. Look at his big strong body! The Romans believed that Neptune created a horse from the Earth with a single blow of his trident.

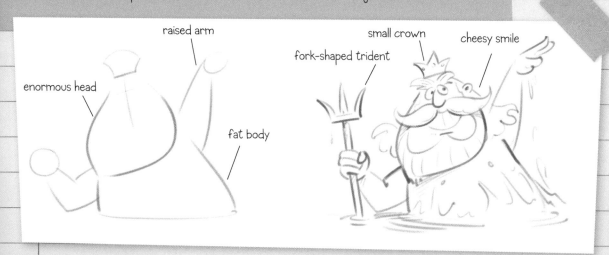

raised arm

small crown

cheesy smile

fork-shaped trident

enormous head

fat body

356 Atlas

The world really does rest on his shoulders! Poor Atlas is bent over and puffed out. He makes the stars revolve by turning the heavens on their axis. Wow! That must be an exhausting job!

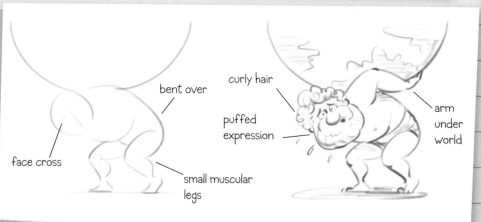

bent over

curly hair

puffed expression

arm under world

face cross

small muscular legs

139

Gladiators

Gladiators were men recruited from the ranks of criminals, slaves and prisoners of war and trained to fight. They were used to entertain the masses who attended the colosseum, having been promised a spectacular battle.

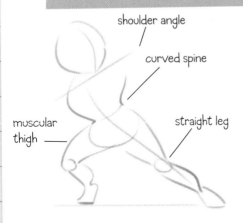

shoulder angle

curved spine

muscular thigh

straight leg

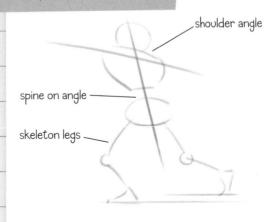

shoulder angle

spine on angle

skeleton legs

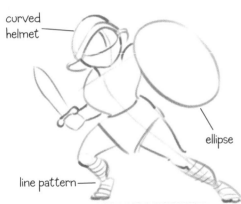

curved helmet

ellipse

line pattern

muscular form

back view

muscular legs

crest

criss-cross pattern

emblem

357

face hidden

trident behind

wavy shape

358

Shield, helmet and sword

A gladiator is built around shapes. The angles and sharp corners drawn to construct this gear help to define its metallic qualities. The decorative detail sets off these period pieces.

359

360

361

362 Colosseum

The Colosseum has 80 arched entrances, which allowed 55 thousand spectators to enter. It is a shaped like a huge ellipse and is 188 metres (617 feet) long and 156 metres (512 feet) wide. Gladiators went into battle against each other and against wild animals in this huge arena.

1 Draw a cake shape that is curved on the top and bottom and straight on the sides. Draw a thin line just inside the top edge, then a straight line in the middle with a curved line either side.

2 Draw pairs of vertical lines down the building. Draw the middle pair first, then the others, making them closer together towards the edges. Sketch the arched windows.

3 Draw the short line pattern around the top then add little spikes above. Add a dot pattern underneath. Shade medium-grey tone inside the arched windows. Add the shadow and you are ready for battle!

TIP

Check out Perspective and 3D on page 30 of the introduction to learn more about creating a 3D form!

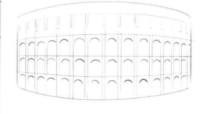

KINGS AND QUEENS

A kingdom is a place where kings and queens rule the land, princesses fall in love with princes and knights save the day with amazing acts of bravery. Imagine being showered in jewels, making important decisions and eating whatever you liked! Royal life wouldn't always be easy, though. You couldn't just pop down to the shops unnoticed!

363 King Edward

All of his subjects love this regal and distinguished-looking king. He takes his role as ruler of all the land very seriously. He is noble and powerful, reigns with fairness in his heart and always shows strength.

1 Draw his large, oval-shaped head on an angle with a face line. Add his big, squarish body. Sketch his leg shapes, slightly crossed.

2 Draw his bulbous nose, ears and beard, leaving a space for his smile. Draw his cloak draping over his shoulders, then add his arm shapes. Define his boots.

3 Draw his eyes and dark eyebrows then add detail to his ear, hair and beard. Add his fingers and put the staff in his hand. Draw his sash and waistband then add his medallions. Add details and shading to his clothing, then bow before the king!

364 **365**

Throne and crown

Where would our king be without his royal throne and crown? He'd be laughed out of the kingdom if he ruled from a recliner and wore a cap! The curves, jewels and decorative detail make this throne and crown look extra special.

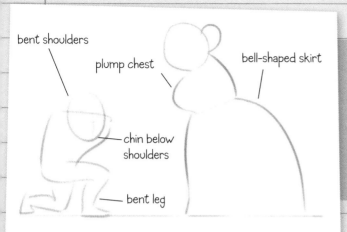

bent shoulders

plump chest

bell-shaped skirt

chin below shoulders

bent leg

366 Queen Victoria

Our plump queen has the important duty of granting this brave fellow his knighthood. He must bend before her so she can touch each of his shoulders with a sword. Rise, Sir Paul!

TIP

Check out Facial Expressions on page 6 of the introduction to learn more about expressing emotion!

arm across chest

spiral bun

looking down

holding helmet

Princess eating escargot

Escargot may be a meal fit for a princess, but seriously? Snails? She is not amused! Facial expression is so important when trying to show emotion. Look how shocked and grossed out she is!

367

368

369 Knight

A knight serves the kingdom, protecting the land from enemy invaders. A knight must be ready for battle at any moment.

1 Draw the knight's head with face cross, adding the helmet shape around the outside. Draw his rounded shoulders, chest and hips.

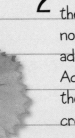

2 Draw his arms followed by the glove shapes. Draw his nose over the cross and add the tip of his helmet. Add his front leg and boot then follow with the leg that crosses behind.

3 Draw his eyes either side of the cross then add his hairy moustache. Draw the pattern across the front of his helmet and add the feather. Add the spear to his hand then draw soft details and shading.

Protection

A knight will not be able to protect himself properly without his trusty sword and shield. Their gear has its own specific detail and emblems. Try drawing this sword and shield, then have a go at creating your own design.

370

371

372 Friar

This jolly friar is a godly person who is at the service of the king and queen. He leads a simple life, providing guidance and support to those in need. He also relies on the charity of others.

face cross

plump body

holding book

happy expression

looking down

long cape

373 Castle

The royal castle is a sight to behold. Many admire its conical rooftops, wavy flags, turrets and arched drawbridge. It is a grand building, fit for royalty.

conical rooftops

turret

small windows

arch

drawbridge

moat

374 Jester

Hear ye, hear ye! The jester is in court! He's making a spectacle of himself shaking his noisy instruments, telling silly jokes and dancing a merry jig. With that crazy outfit, he should be thrown in the dungeon!

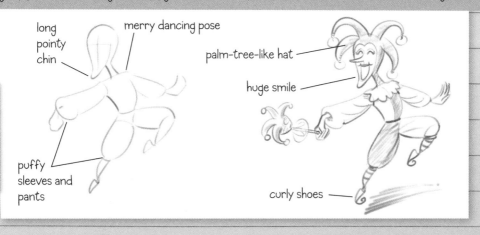

long pointy chin

merry dancing pose

palm-tree-like hat

huge smile

puffy sleeves and pants

curly shoes

NEW FRONTIERS

The Wild West was a time during American colonial history. It was a period that included war with Native Americans and the formation of new colonial settlements. People, including outlaws, were blazing trails on horseback across the harsh desert. Some of the most famous legends of this time were Jesse James, Billy the Kid, Belle Starr and Wyatt Earp.

375

Classic cowboy

Yee-ha! Go get 'em, cowboy! He's getting ready to muster some cattle. With his lasso at the ready and on his trusty horse, he's pushing forward, chasing down a runaway cow.

1 Draw the stretched-out shapes for the horse's head and neck, then follow with his curved body. Draw the cowboy's big head over the horse's neck. Add his body shape and legs.

2 Draw the horse's stretched-out legs. Add the front legs, then the ones behind. Draw the cowboy's arms, define his hat and outfit and then add the saddle.

3 Draw the face of the cowboy. Add his hair, ear and vest. Draw his checked shirt, belt and lasso. Draw the horse's face and ears, and his wavy mane and tail. Add the girdle and straps, and some shading, and away they gallop!

Fun variations

You've got to be ready for trouble in the Wild West. You should always be on the lookout for outlaws approaching and varmints in hiding – even in your tin cup! Have a bit of fun with your subjects. Don't be afraid to put them in different scenarios!

376

377

378 Sheriff

There'd be no social order if it weren't for the local lawmen. This sheriff is ready to take on the outlaws. With that big badge and his bow-legged stance, he'll show them who's boss!

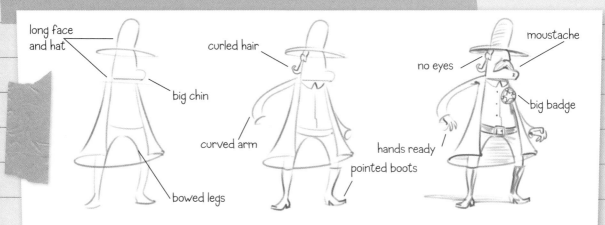

long face and hat
curled hair
moustache
no eyes
big chin
curved arm
big badge
hands ready
pointed boots
bowed legs

zigzag pattern
little eyes and nose
big smile
big head
large round sombrero
guitar shape

379 Mexican amigo

Arriba! This happy amigo is playing you a cheerful tune on his guitar. With his big sombrero and moustache, this roving troubadour likes to serenade the locals to keep them out of trouble!

380 Annie Oakley

Annie travels with Buffalo Bill's Wild West show. She's a sharp-shooting talented superstar of the stage. A fun-loving character, she'll kick up her heels at any opportunity.

curved hat
puffy hair
spinning lasso
straight shoulders
excited expression
wavy skirt shape
bent arms
foot points up

381 Apache brave

This Apache doesn't suffer fools gladly. He's in a guarded pose – his face looks serious and his arms are crossed. He loves his people and wants to protect his land.

1 Draw his head with a face cross and big jaw. Sketch his big chest and the outlines of his large arms. Draw the bottom of his top and his straight legs.

2 Add his headband and long hair, then define the details of his top. Add the two feather shapes behind his arm and draw his moccasin boots.

3 Draw his serious eyes, big nose and mouth over the face cross. Draw the fine texture of his hair and add the details of his headband. Add fringing to his top and his hand bump. Darken and define the outline and add a light shadow below.

 TIP Check out Designing a Character on page 26 of the introduction to learn more about setting the scene!

Home on the range

This Apache needs his trusty bow and arrow to hunt for his supper, and somewhere to go home to after a hard day on the land. Don't be afraid to set the scene for your characters by including other objects in your picture.

382

383

384 Cactus

You know you're done for if you're stuck in the desert with no water for miles. But wait! There's a spiky, weird-looking cactus up ahead. You can drink cactus juice to keep you hydrated!

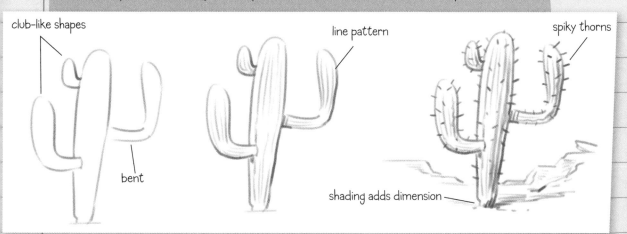

club-like shapes

bent

line pattern

shading adds dimension

spiky thorns

385 Pocahontas

A beautiful Native American princess, Pocahontas was strong-willed, brave and a free spirit. She saved an Englishman, Captain John Smith, from execution. She also had the secret name Matoaka.

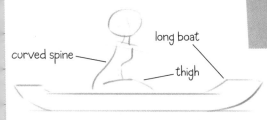

curved spine

long boat

thigh

hair moving

happy expression

paddle in water

386 Coyote

This wild dog is found in the deserts of North and Central America. At night, by the light of the moon, they let out a series of high-pitched cries and short yips. It is the true sound of the west.

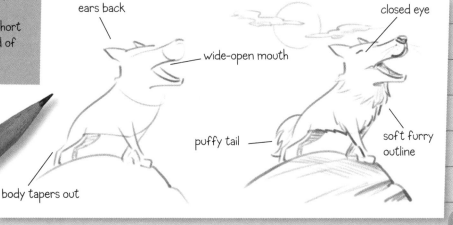

ears back

wide-open mouth

closed eye

puffy tail

soft furry outline

body tapers out

149

TRANSPORT THROUGH TIME

Planes, trains and automobiles! Over the years transport has changed rapidly, giving us many different ways to get from A to B. The evolution of transport has progressed from the slow and steady camel to the super-fast Ferrari. Who knows, maybe one day we will be taking shuttles to the moon!

387

Steam train

This old steam train is going up the hill as fast as he can. Coal is being loaded into his furnace as he releases puffs of smoke and steam into the air. The train has left the station! Toot, toot!

1 Draw the curved baseline of the train then add the cylinder shape for the front. Follow with the box shapes for the engine room and the middle and end carriages.

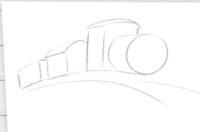

2 Draw the curved grate at the front followed by the four oval wheels. Add the smoke stack and the window behind. Define the line of the track.

3 Add his circle nose, smile and eyes. Draw the arch window and six small wheels. Add detail to the carriages and front engine. Draw the tracks and the puffs of smoke, then add shading. Chugga, chugga, off he goes!

Changes over time

Before there were motor cars, humans used animals to get around. These two scenes couldn't be more different. A sheikh moving slowly through the hot, dry desert and a lady, protected from the elements, being driven to her destination.

388

389

390 Hot air balloon

Humans are an inventive bunch. After many attempts, the first manned balloon aircraft took off from Paris, France in 1783. These people look like they're blowing a little off course!

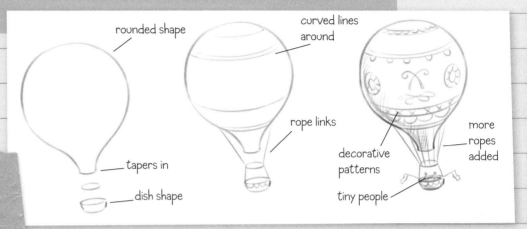

rounded shape

curved lines around

tapers in

dish shape

rope links

decorative patterns

tiny people

more ropes added

391 Biplane

The biplane signified a revolution in aviation history – it was the most successful aircraft design of the early 1900s. With an open cockpit, pilots had to wear goggles and warm clothing for protection.

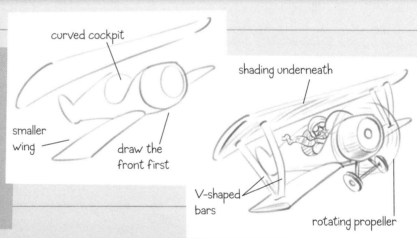

curved cockpit

smaller wing

draw the front first

shading underneath

V-shaped bars

rotating propeller

392 Zeppelin

Count Ferdinand von Zeppelin invented the airship in the late 1800s. Its first manned flight was taken in 1900. Zeppelin airships were used in the bombing of London during World War I, but were easily shot down because they were too slow.

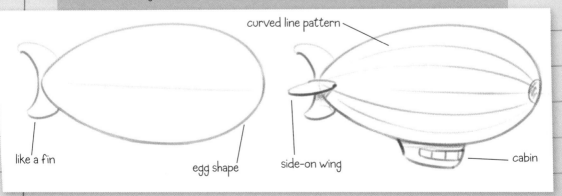

curved line pattern

like a fin

egg shape

side-on wing

cabin

393 Ford Model T

Production of the Ford Model T began on 12 August, 1908. It had gas lamps, optional windshield and cost $850. The final Model T ran off the production line in 1927.

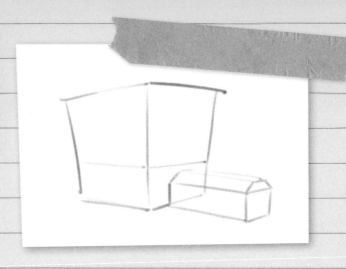

1 Draw a box-shaped cabin with the roof and base on opposing angles. Draw a coffin shape for the bonnet area.

2 Draw the curved inside of the car. Add the dashboard and rooftop. Draw the base of the chassis so you can add the three oval wheels.

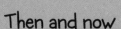

3 Draw the man's head, then his body, then add the lady. Add the circular lights, the fenders and the running board along the side. Add further details, shading and the background, and you're ready to go! Honk, honk!

394

395

Then and now

How things have changed, from the slightly awkward motion of the penny-farthing to the smooth and streamlined design of the modern bicycle. Check out the difference between the bike shapes and the position of the riders' spines.

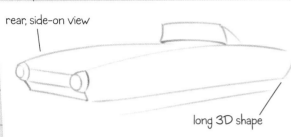

rear, side-on view

long 3D shape

396 Classic Cadillac

The space age has arrived! The 1950s saw the dawn of a new era in automobile design. People wanted a more modern-looking style, and the Cadillac's rocket-shaped fenders were a hit!

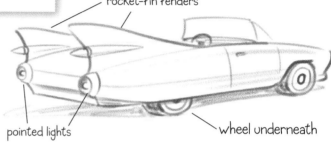

rocket-fin fenders

pointed lights

wheel underneath

397

VW Beetle

Volkswagen began production of its classic economy car in 1938. Dubbed the 'VW Bug', it had the boot in the front and the engine in the back. The design platform used for the Volkswagen Beetle is the longest-running and most-manufactured in the world.

TIP Check out Perspective and 3D on page 30 of the introduction to learn more about perspective!

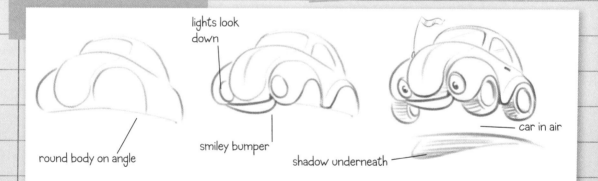

lights look down

round body on angle

smiley bumper

shadow underneath

car in air

sleek design

large wheels

398 Ferrari

Vroom, vroom! The Italian Ferrari is one of the fastest cars in the world. Much-admired for its look and speed, this car has dominated car-racing championships around the world.

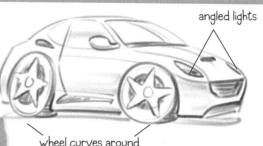

angled lights

wheel curves around

FASHION THROUGH THE AGES

Since the early 1900s fashion has gone through many changes. Each decade has been influenced by the movies, art, music and events of its time. From the suave top hat and tails of the 1920s to the grungy look of the 1990s, people have been eager to embrace current trends or simply to stand out from the crowd. So buckle up and put on your best outfit – you're in for a ride!

399 1920s gent

Smart and sophisticated, the top hat and tails marked the 1920s. Gentlemen were expected to dress a certain way for a night out on the town.

1 Draw his round head, chin and neck. Draw his large chest on an angle then add his thick A-shaped legs and small shoes on the same angle.

2 Draw his arm shapes, then add his hands. Define his face shape and his shoes, then add his top hat.

3 Draw his simple face and ear, followed by his jacket opening and lapels. Draw his vest and tie, define his hands and add his walking stick. Darken and define the outline then add shading. What a jolly old chap!

The 30s and 40s

After World War I, glamour was all the rage. Hollywood began to make its mark. Then wartime came again, the world was running out of resources and fashion became more practical. Just look at the differences between these two gals!

on a lean

petite features

hourglass figure

head turned

boyish pose

ove

hands in pockets

400 1930s Hollywood

401 1940s wartime

402

1950s rocker girl

The 1950s saw the dawn of a new age. After World War II, people were sick of going without. Young people wanted to be free and kick up their heels. Check out this girl's fun poodle skirt!

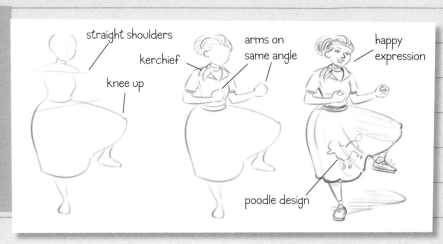

straight shoulders

kerchief

knee up

arms on same angle

happy expression

poodle design

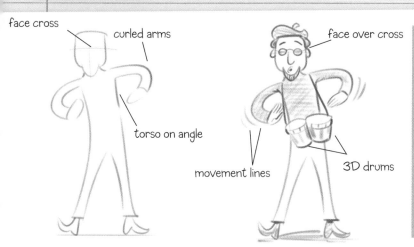

face cross

curled arms

torso on angle

face over cross

movement lines

3D drums

403

1950s beatnik

Beatniks were part of a literary generation called 'The Beat Generation'. They considered themselves to be very cool, and moved to the beat of their own drum. Too cool for school!

404 1960s flower power

Groovy man! Flower power was all about love. Psychedelic colours and patterns were all the rage. Short skirts, flower garlands and peace signs signified change.

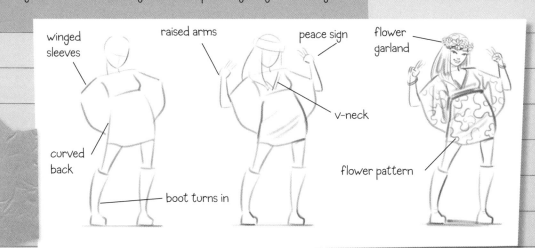

winged sleeves

raised arms

peace sign

flower garland

curved back

v-neck

boot turns in

flower pattern

405

1970s funky lady

This disco dazzler is getting down to the beat. With her groovy afro, flared jeans and platform shoes, she is ready to dance the night away. Look at her go!

1 Draw her curved face and neck. Add a face cross and the round shape of her hair. Draw her chest and hips, then draw the shape of her flared pants in an open pose. Add her shoes.

2 Draw her happy expression over the face cross and add the fuzzy outline of her hair. Draw her hoop earrings, then her arms and open palms. Add a stripy pattern to her top, draw her belt and define her platform shoes. Add some shading and she's ready to boogie!

406 1970s disco guy

Boogie wonderland! Silk shirts with big pointy collars were all the rage in the 70s. This guy's got all the smooth moves. Saturday night is all right because he's lost in the music.

flared sleeves

spine line

bent leg

curly hairstyle

big pointy collar

pointing finger

happy expression

vest

1970s punk

There's anarchy around the world. The 70s saw the arrival of punk – a movement that rebelled against a conservative lifestyle. Young people wanted to dress outrageously and listen to punk rock music.

407
- face cross
- open jacket
- short skirt
- short hairstyle
- choker

408
- angry pose
- head down
- hands on hips
- spiky mohawk
- angry expression
- tattoos

409 1980s new wave

Electropop music has arrived – and so has bad 80s fashion! Music was laced with electronic sounds and girls wore puffy skirts, fishnets and permed hair.

- curved body
- wide skirt shape
- feet turn in

- curly hair
- puffy skirt
- fishnet stockings

410 1990s grunge

A new style of music and fashion was born out of the need for an alternative way of being. It all began in a place called Seattle, in the United States. Boys grew their hair long, wore flannel shirts and rocked out to bands like Nirvana.

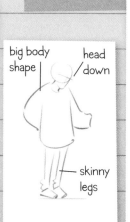
- big body shape
- head down
- skinny legs

- long hair
- downward gaze
- checked shirt

TIP Check out Designing a Character on page 26 of the introduction to learn more about dressing a character!

EXTINCT ANIMALS

Since the beginning of time, some of the Earth's strangest creatures have become extinct. The dodo bird, the woolly mammoth and Steller's sea cow, just to name a few, have either been eliminated because of changes in climate or through hunting by humans. Today, there are still many endangered species that are in danger of becoming extinct.

411

Woolly mammoth

This prehistoric creature is in a bit of a hurry! Perhaps he's looking for his next leafy snack? Check out his long, hairy coat and huge trunk and tusks. What a curious creature!

1 Draw his curved body shape and a bump for his head. Add his long, curly trunk, making it thicker at the top.

2 Draw the hole for his tusk, then add his eyebrows and floppy ear. Add chunky, short legs under his body.

3 Draw his curved eyes, big curly tusks and smiley mouth. Add the soft, hairy lines for his coat and draw his tail. Darken and define his outline and add the soft shadow beneath. Off he goes!

Cute animals

The little ones are at play! When drawing cute creatures like this baby mammoth and young dodo, try putting them in a cute or energetic pose. To help capture their age, give them oversized features, like a big head.

412

413

414 Tasmanian tiger

Are they alive or extinct? That is the million-dollar question. Many people believe that this sneaky creature still exists, evading humans by hiding in the wilderness.

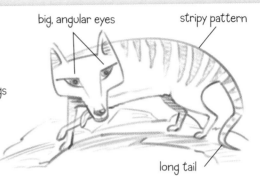

big, angular eyes

stripy pattern

long tail

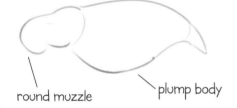

curve

small thin legs

curved baseline

415 Steller's sea cow

This enormous, plump marine creature was closely related to the dugong and lived in the northern Pacific region. Being a herbivore, this sea cow liked to munch on kelp.

fins curl over

wrinkles

round muzzle

plump body

416 Sabre-toothed tiger

This ferocious carnivore is in a grumpy mood. Watch out for those deadly canines – he means business! His arms are crossed and he has a strong stance.

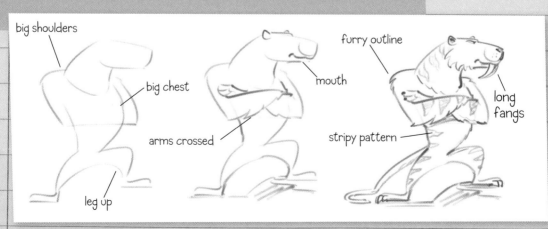

big shoulders

big chest

arms crossed

leg up

furry outline

mouth

long fangs

stripy pattern

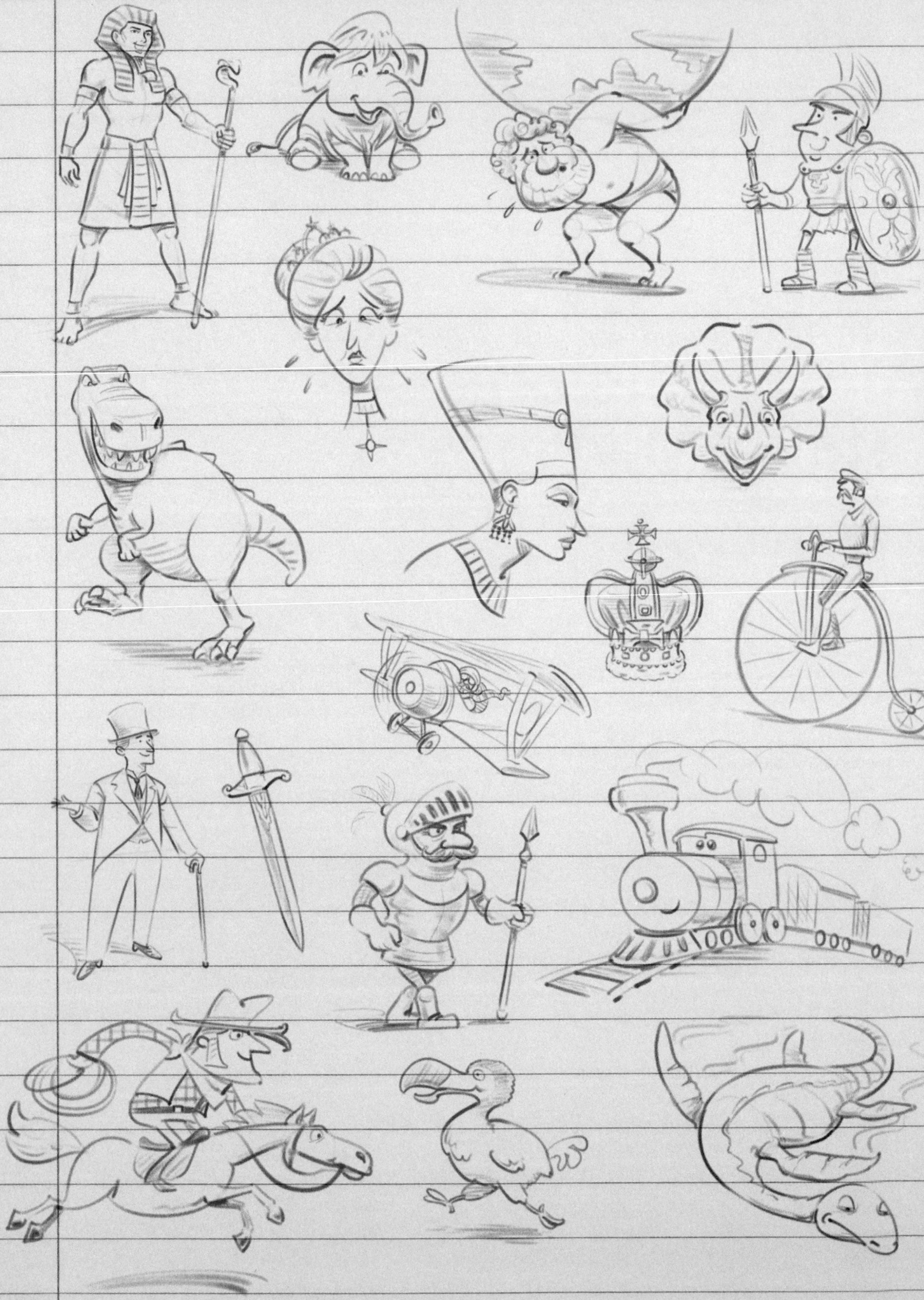

OLYMPICS

The first Olympic Games were held in Ancient Greece in 776 BC. That makes them nearly 3000 years old! In ancient times they included sports such as boxing, running, javelin, shot-put, long jump and equestrian events. Fast-forward to today and the Olympics is a huge affair with many events. Countries from all over the world compete and people cheer like crazy for their own nation.

417 Sprinter

On your marks, get set, go! Sprinting is all about speed and achieving the correct running action. A runner's power is determined by the strength of their legs.

1 Draw the runner's head on an angle, and his curved spine. Form his chest around the spine and add his arm bent behind. Add his muscular front leg and then the one behind. Draw the baseline below.

2 Draw his hair, ear and neck, then his bent front arm with the palm facing up. Draw his calf muscles and small feet.

3 Shape the profile of his face and add fingers to the hand shapes. Add the lines of his running outfit and define his shoes. Darken and define the outline of his muscular form. Add light shading and a shadow beneath, then he's off!

418 Starting pose

Your runner's muscular body takes on a different form when he launches himself off the starting blocks. Observe the definition in his muscles and the line of his spine and back leg.

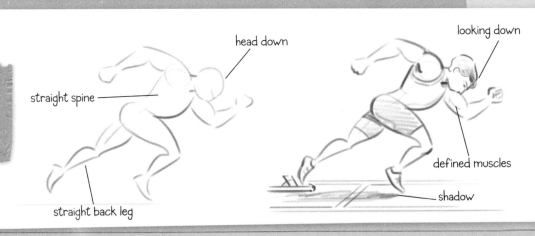

head down
straight spine
straight back leg
looking down
defined muscles
shadow

419 High jumper

The action used in high jumping is called the 'Fosbury Flop'. This style of jumping was first used in the 1968 Olympics by an American named Dick Fosbury. He won gold, and the rest is history!

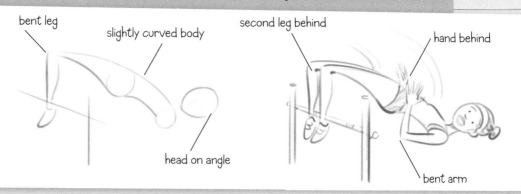

bent leg

slightly curved body

second leg behind

hand behind

head on angle

bent arm

420 Javelin thrower

Javelin originates back in Ancient Greece, where it appeared in the first Olympic games. A spear-like rod is pulled back behind the thrower as they run, and then released.

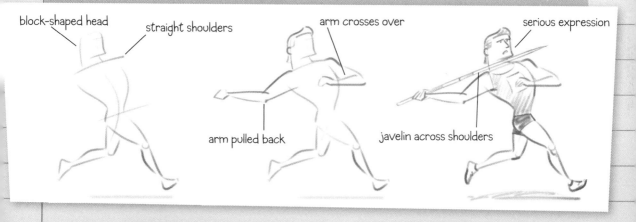

block-shaped head

straight shoulders

arm crosses over

serious expression

arm pulled back

javelin across shoulders

421

422

Discus and shot-put

Discus and shot-put throwers use their whole body to launch the shot. Observe their solid, muscular forms and the angle of their shoulders and arms.

163

423 Swimmer

Being a top-rate swimmer requires serious dedication and lots of early-morning practice sessions. A swimmer's body must be in optimal shape so it can propel them through the pool at record-breaking speeds!

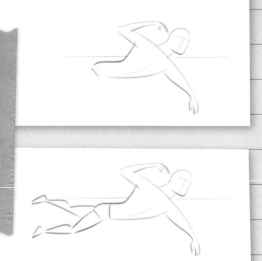

1 Draw the swimmer's angular head with face cross and a thick neck. Draw his wide shoulders on an angle, with one arm bent and the other pointing straight down. Add his wide chest and thin hips. Draw the water line behind.

2 Under the water line, draw his small bottom with swim trunks, then add his muscular legs and pointed feet. Draw the front leg first, followed by the one behind.

3 Draw his face over the cross, then add his swimming cap and ears. Add his fingers and define his chest muscles. Define and darken the outline of his form. Lightly add the waves of the water and the movement and splashes. Go for gold!

424 Gymnast

Gymnasts bend, twist, flip and contort their bodies in amazing ways! A gymnast has to be lithe, strong and flexible in order to push their body to the limit. They also need great balance.

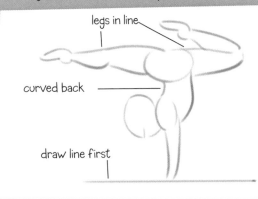

legs in line

curved back

draw line first

arm behind

balance beam

happy expression

Diver

This female diver is seen in a three-stage sequence. She begins the tumble section of her dive, then she turns her body to begin the descent into the water before finally entering the pool. Observe the perspective her body is seen from, and her muscular form.

425

426

427

428 Weightlifter

This heavyweight of the weightlifting circuit has really got his hands full! His face is showing his desperation and determination to push that barbell up over his head. He's in the perfect position, but can he stand up?

TIP

Check out Facial Expressions on page 6 of the introduction to learn more about importance of expression!

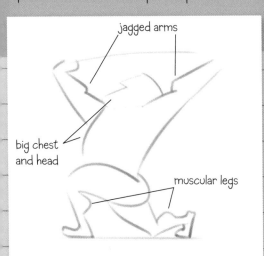

jagged arms

big chest and head

muscular legs

bar is bending

desperate expression

3D weights

PLAY BALL

People love their sport, especially anything involving a ball! Whether it is a tennis ball, football or basketball, we love kicking, hitting and throwing them all over the place. Ball games are believed to have existed in ancient times, when the Romans and Greeks both played sports similar to football and soccer. So join in, grab a ball and be a part of the team. Let's play ball!

429 Soccer player

Soccer, also known as football, is called 'the world game', as it is played by millions of people from different cultures around the world. Fans say it is very poetic to watch because of the precision passing and incredible footwork.

1 Draw the soccer player's t-shirt nipping in at the waist on a slight angle. Add his big shorts and a short baseline underneath.

2 Draw his thick neck and head on a slight angle then add his face cross. Add both of his arms. Draw his front leg against the baseline, then draw the other leg bent up behind.

3 Draw his face over the cross. Gently shade the details of his clothing and shoes. Darken and define his outline, then add the soccer ball over the tip of his shoe. Now add the grass and he's ready to pass!

Different moves

Your soccer player can bend it like Beckham! He's a fierce shot for goal and can launch a ball into full flight. Check out his teammate's wicked headshot. His grimacing face shows his determination.

430

431

432 Basketballer

This guy's certainly got some cool moves on the basketball court. Look at that slam dunk! His legs are wide apart, his arm curled around and his eye on the hoop. Go you good thing!

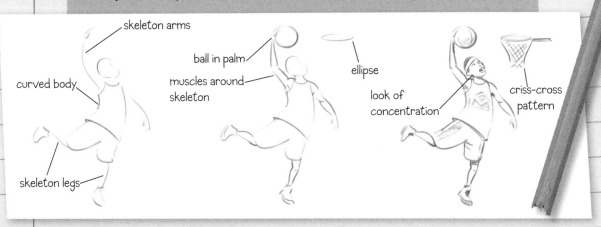

skeleton arms

ball in palm

ellipse

curved body

muscles around skeleton

look of concentration

criss-cross pattern

skeleton legs

433 Quarterback

The quarterback is about to make his move. The pack is descending upon him so he must launch the ball forward. He's got his helmet and padding on for protection, and his powerful throwing arm is ready for action.

start at helmet

helmet guard

open palm

side-on view

A-shaped legs

add shadow

434 Volleyballer

Indoors or outdoors? Volleyball is an all-weather sport. Look at this girl go, launching into her set shot with great vigour. Her legs are elevated, her arm is pulled back and her eye is directly on the ball.

straight arm

arm pulled back

legs on same angle

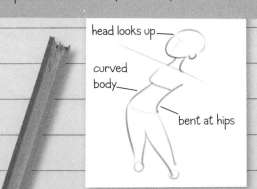

head looks up

curved body

bent at hips

167

435 Baseball pitcher

A baseball pitcher is a highly valued member of a baseball team. The pitcher's speed and precision can turn a game on its head. Check out this guy's powerful pose. His leg and arms are on a severe angle, his spine is curved and his head is pushed forward.

1 Draw his head shape with a face cross and his curved, wide torso on an angle. Draw his bent leg, then add the mound beneath him. Draw his straight leg as an extension of his body.

2 Draw his cap and ear. Sketch the sleeve of his top. Add his front arm, the ball and then the arm behind.

3 Draw his face over the cross. Darken and define his outline and his clothing and shoes. Softly shade his clothing and the mound beneath. Now release the curve ball!

436 Batter

This batter's reactions are lightning quick. He's out to hit a home run and the opposition know it. Look at his brooding and dark expression. He means business. With his curved back and cap down he's ready to go!

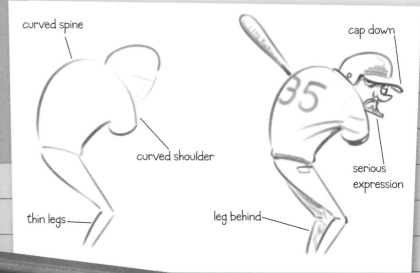

curved spine

cap down

curved shoulder

serious expression

thin legs

leg behind

437

Fast bowler

Anyone for cricket? This game originates from 16th century England and is now played around the world. This fast bowler has a pretty mean action. I wouldn't want to be on the receiving end of that ball!

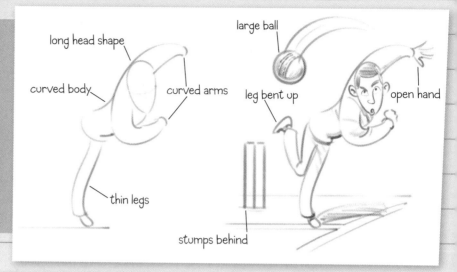

long head shape

curved body

curved arms

thin legs

large ball

leg bent up

open hand

stumps behind

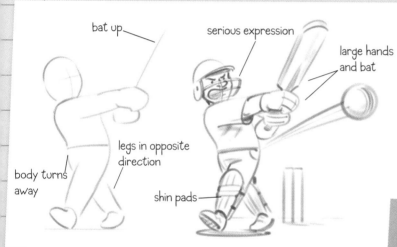

bat up

serious expression

large hands and bat

body turns away

legs in opposite direction

shin pads

438 Batsman

This guy's not going out for a duck today. He was ready for that fast ball. Check out his wicked swing. His large arms have elevated that bat and it looks like he's hit it for six!

TIP

Check out Action and Poses on page 10 of the introduction to learn more about dynamic movement!

439

Tennis player

Wimbledon, here we come! With a double-handed backhand this girl is going to power through that ball. Her racquet is extended behind, her feet are apart and her body is leaning forward. She's going to be a superstar!

arm back

body bent forward

open legs

eyes down

hands wrap around

racquet back

HOT WHEELS

Vroom! Vroom! Go, greased lightning! The sound of a racing car or motorbike revving its engine sends excitement pumping through the veins. People that are obsessed with motor sports are called 'rev heads'. The cars are hotting up and the smell of petrol is in the air. Let the action begin!

440 Formula One

The first Formula One championship race was held at Silverstone in the United Kingdom in 1950. Huge advances have been made since then. The modern-day Formula One car has the benefit of cutting-edge technology, making the car aerodynamic and faster than ever!

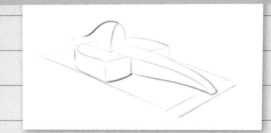

1 Draw the 3D shape of the car on an angle. Start with the cockpit, then add the sides and the long, pointed bonnet. Draw the rectangular outline around the car's body.

2 Draw the winged spoiler at the back, then the back wheel. Draw the steering wheel in front of the cockpit and add the wheels either side of the bonnet.

3 Add the winged bumper to the front of the car. Draw circular hubcaps and add detail to the car's body and bonnet. Add wings to the spoiler. Softly add shading to give the car dimension.

441 Cartoon racing car

She's a beauty! This car is ahead of the pack and on track to win the championship. The movement lines show how fast she's going. She's as happy as can be, zooming off towards the finish line.

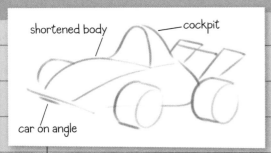

shortened body

cockpit

car on angle

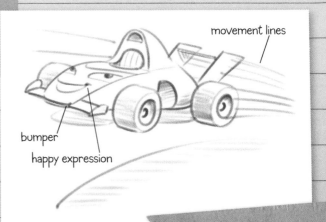

movement lines

bumper

happy expression

442 NASCAR

NASCAR stands for the National Association for Stock Car Auto Racing. Stock cars race around large oval tracks and can reach speeds of over 320 km per hour (200 mph).

long 3D wedge shape

squared off

cabin sits on top

spoiler added

443 Rally car

Rallying is a type of car racing that happens on private or public roads. Instead of driving around a circuit, rallying measures the time taken to drive between various points.

curved top and back

flat bottom

rounded front

wheel arches

smiley grille and lights

3D wheels

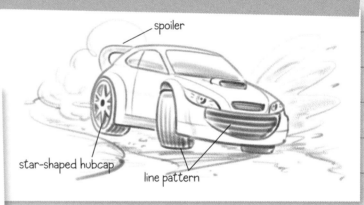

spoiler

star-shaped hubcap

line pattern

444 Dragster

This top fuel dragster goes from 0 to 160 km per hour (100 mph) in 0.7 seconds. That's super fast! Dragsters run on a mixture of nitro methane and methanol, and resemble an exaggerated version of a Formula One car.

wings

body on angle

enlarged back wheels

engine

fire

tiny front wheels

445 Superbike

The first superbike was created in the late *1960s* by Honda. People were stunned by the power of the bike and in the early *1970s* they began to race the superbike. The superbike championships began in *1988*.

1 Draw the 3D round wheel, then draw the bike's body and the shield on an angle.

3 Draw the bike's handle, then the axle over the wheel. Draw the V-shaped detail on the bike's shield. Add the wavy outline of the shadow beneath, then the soft shading. Off he races! Vroom!

2 Draw the bike's window and handle shaft. Follow with the rider's helmet, shoulders and arms, drawing them all on an angle. Draw the rider's bent leg out to the side of the bike. Add light shading around his waist.

446 Harley Davidson

Known as the preferred ride of bikers, a Harley Davidson is a heavy bike with a black enamelled body and silver fittings. Harley riders are often seen cruising the highways in a procession of bikes.

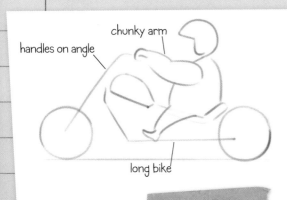

chunky arm

handles on angle

long bike

long beard

fender

spokes

447 Sprint car

Sprint cars race around circular tracks, reaching speeds of up to 230 km per hour (140 mph). The wings on top of the car make it easier to control and reduce the risk of the car becoming airborne.

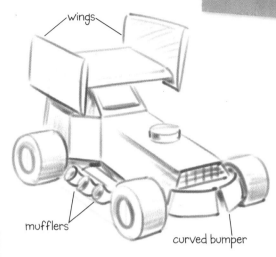

wings

mufflers

curved bumper

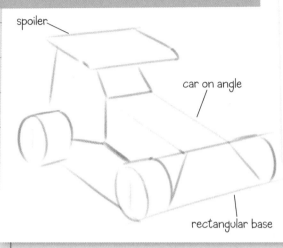

spoiler

car on angle

rectangular base

448 Circuit racing

Now you've drawn one sprint car, try drawing three of them on a circuit. On the left, observe the different 3D shape for each car. Notice how they change in size from back to front, and that they are all on different angles. Start by drawing the smallest one, then work your way forward.

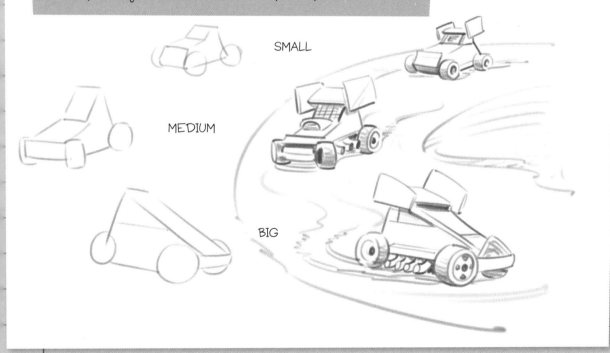

SMALL

MEDIUM

BIG

UP IN THE CLOUDS

For centuries, human beings have been fascinated by the idea of flight and being as free as a bird, flying among the clouds and looking down on Earth. The famous painter and inventor Leonardo Da Vinci said, 'When once you have tasted flight, you will forever walk the Earth with your eyes turned skyward, for there you have been, and there you will always long to return.'

449

Aerobatics

Aerobatics is the art of flying and moving an aircraft in a series of sequences that involve spinning, rotating and rolling. For most people, this is a sickening thought!

1 Draw the outline of the plane's body on an angle, then the outline of the cockpit. Draw the seat inside.

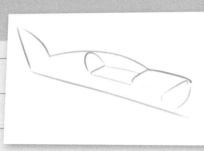

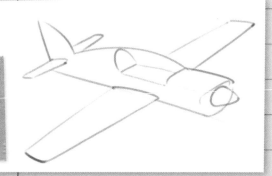

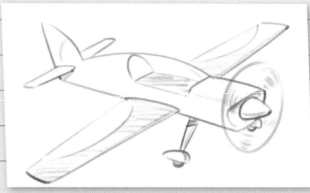

2 Draw the wings either side of the cockpit. Observe how one wing is smaller than the other one. Draw a cone shape for the middle of the propeller and add the little wings either side of the tail.

3 Draw the plane's landing gear and wheels (one is hiding behind the propeller), then lightly draw the oval movement lines for the propeller. Softly add the details and shading on the plane's body. We're ready for take-off!

Manoeuvres

This plane has got more moves to attempt. Try drawing your plane turning and rolling. The plane on the left is seen from underneath and the one on the right is seen from above. Notice how the wings look different in each drawing.

450

451

452 Spitfire

This high-performance, short-range fighter was used throughout World War II. Check him out! He looks pretty angry and ready for battle. I wouldn't want to get in his line of fire!

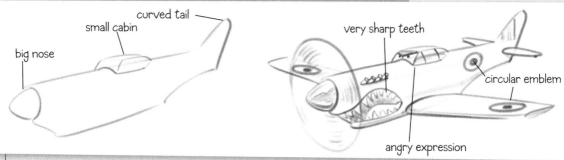

big nose

small cabin

curved tail

very sharp teeth

circular emblem

angry expression

453 Fighter jet

This military aircraft has a superior design and can hold two basic air-to-air missiles. Its streamlined body is built for speed and the two jets at the back thrust it forwards through the atmosphere.

straight edge

pointed nose

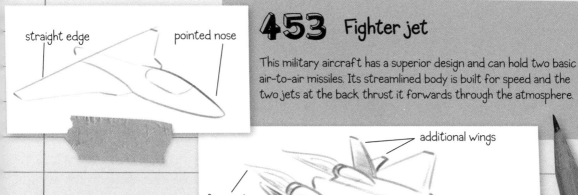

additional wings

fiery jets

454 Stealth bomber

This aircraft uses stealth technology, which interferes with radar systems to avoid detection by the enemy. Examples of stealth aircraft include the Nighthawk, Lightning and Raptor.

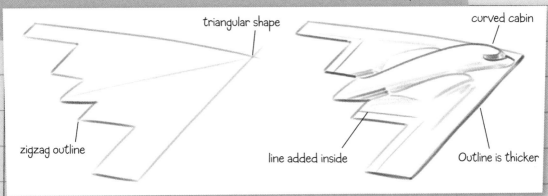

triangular shape

curved cabin

zigzag outline

line added inside

Outline is thicker

455 Rescue helicopter

This very important aircraft, and the personnel that operate it, performs dangerous rescues both on land and at sea. So if you ever get lost, there will be someone to save you!

1 Draw the curved body of the helicopter and the flat base that can be seen from underneath. Add the front window and the bent tail.

2 On top of the helicopter, add the three layered shapes for the base of the propeller. Draw the rectangular side doors and the side wings, then add the broken ellipse for the propeller's outline.

3 Draw the large propellers on top and the small tail propellers. Draw wheels under the side wings, then add the rope and the person being rescued. Sketch the choppy waves, then go over the picture, adding further details and shading.

Cartoon helicopter

This regular little helicopter can be determined or apprehensive. Check out the exaggerated expressions on his face. He's super cute, with his small, rounded body and short tail. Try drawing him with other expressions.

456
Determined

457
Apprehensive

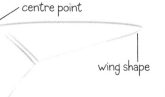

centre point

wing shape

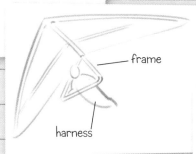

frame

harness

458 Hang-gliding

Humans' fascination with flight led them to invent the hang-glider. It's the closest we can get to flying like a bird. Hang-gliders launch themselves off mountains to begin their flight.

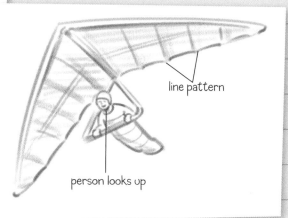

line pattern

person looks up

459 Glider

Gliders have no engine and are commonly launched by a small powered plane, which is attached to the glider by a rope. The glider pilot releases the rope when they reach the perfect altitude.

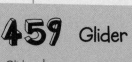

body on angle   cabin

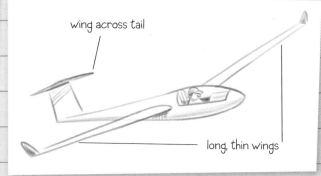

wing across tail

long, thin wings

460 Skydiving

Most people would never consider attempting such a scary jump, but some love the thrill of freefalling from high up in the clouds. You definitely need a great deal of courage to be a skydiver!

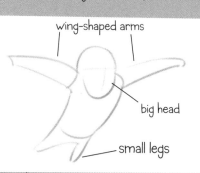

wing-shaped arms

big head

small legs

movement lines

legs bent behind

excited expression

EXTREME SPORTS

Adrenaline junkies around the world love the thrill and risk of extreme sports. Skateboarders do wicked tricks on ramps, bungee jumpers launch themselves off the edge of a bridge and snowboarders descend down steep slopes at high speeds. They must be crazy! Or maybe they just love taking life to the extreme. Gnarly, dude!

461 BMX rider

BMX championships are held off-road, on purpose-built tracks. BMX bikes can be manipulated in a variety of ways, allowing the riders to do tricks and become airborne. Crazy!

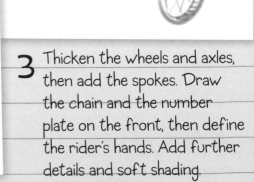

1 Draw the bike's frame and handlebars. Add the circle-shaped wheel at the back, and the front oval wheel.

2 Thicken the bike's frame. Draw the rider's helmet, then add his shoulders and arms, and his hands on the handlebars. Draw his hips and legs, then define the handlebars.

3 Thicken the wheels and axles, then add the spokes. Draw the chain and the number plate on the front, then define the rider's hands. Add further details and soft shading.

BMX tricks

This kid is having fun working out how far he can push his bike! He's fooling around in his backyard, seeing how many tricks he can master. Using strength and balance, he's spinning the bike on its axle and doing a wheelie.

462

463

464 Motocross rider

This rider is speeding around the motocross circuit, desperate to win the championship. He's launched his bike over a jump and is flying toward the finish line!

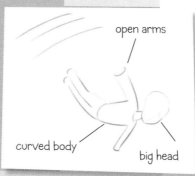

draw chassis first

oval front wheel

mudguard

number added

bent leg

wheel on side

line pattern

bumpy wheel texture

465

Bungee jumper

Bungee jumping is certainly not for the faint-hearted. Throwing yourself off a bridge is a pretty extreme thing to do! This guy's regretting his decision, that's for sure. His expression says it all!

open arms

curved body

big head

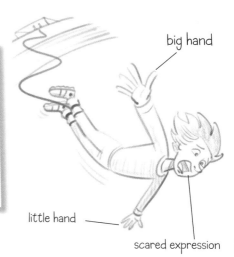

big hand

little hand

scared expression

466 Monster truck

These beasts are pretty comical to look at, but they can be hugely entertaining. Monster trucks are very popular because people love seeing things get smashed up!

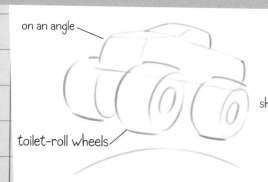

on an angle

toilet-roll wheels

pattern on wheels

shadow underneath

467 Snowboarder

Snowboarding is like a cross between skateboarding and skiing – without wheels or ski poles! Check out this guy doing a jump off a ski slope. Totally awesome!

1 Draw the bottom of the snowboard on an angle. Draw the snowboarder's rounded leg shapes coming out from the middle. Add his chest and arm shapes above his thigh.

2 Draw his head shape and his hood around his neck. Make sure you add his ski goggles. Add his hand fanning outwards, then the edge of his shoes.

3 Draw his nose and smiley mouth, then add his hand wrapping around the board. Add the details of his jacket and pants, and the pattern on his board. Darken and define the whole outline. Add soft shading and the hills below and away he goes!

Skater dudes

Snowboarding isn't the only type of boarding. These skateboarders have some gravity-defying moves – they definitely need lots of power in their legs! These skater dudes can flip their decks and manipulate their bodies in extreme ways.

468

469

470 Ski jumper

This ski jumper is like a human dart with her aerodynamic jumping pose and special clothing. For a jumper to travel a large distance they must launch at great speed off a long ramp so they can propel themselves forward. Yikes!

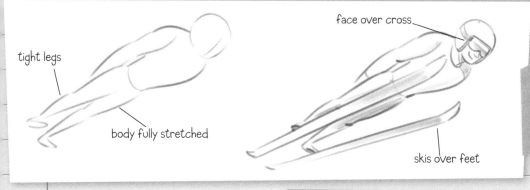

tight legs

body fully stretched

face over cross

skis over feet

471 Snowmobile

Snowmobiles are lots of fun to ride fast through the snow. They are especially handy in remote, cold places with vast amounts of snow, as they can cover huge distances very quickly!

wedge shape

on an angle

pointed head

line across middle

curved shield

leg added

skis added

472 Kayaker

This kayaker is travelling down the fierce rapids, the force of the water propelling him forward. He's airborne! His body is pushed back by the power as his paddle is lifted above his head.

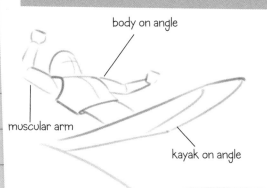

body on angle

muscular arm

kayak on angle

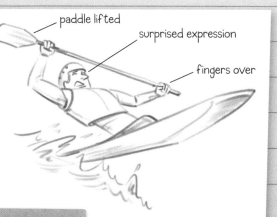

paddle lifted

surprised expression

fingers over

SUPERHEROES

Is it a bird? Is it a plane? No, it's a superhero! The world of comic books is an inventive place filled with weird and wonderful characters. Look out, all you villains and bad guys! With their cape, mask and superpowers, these heroes are ready to strike. BAAM!

473

Caped Crusader

He can leap tall buildings in a single bound and break a car in two with his bare hands. When bad guys see him coming, they run in the other direction. The Caped Crusader's trademarks are his assured smile and massive fists.

1 Draw his angular head and chiselled jaw. Follow with his big shoulders and chest that nips in at the waist. Draw his massive fists and muscular thighs.

2 Draw his wavy cape flapping in different directions. Add his fingers inside the hand shapes, then draw his calves. Sketch the movement line behind him.

3 Draw his confident expression and his hair and ears. Darken and define his outline. Draw the logo on his costume and softly add shading. It's the courageous Caped Crusader!

Caped Crusader – two different ways

The Caped Crusader's pretty vain about his teeth. So much for that winning smile! He's pretty angry now. Even though he's a good guy, he still has a bad temper! Try drawing your crusader showing other emotions.

TIP Check out Head Construction on page 2 of the introduction to learn more about head shape and personality!

474

475

476

Robo Man

Robo Man is half man, half metal – he's unbreakable! Move over, man of steel – this is the real man of the moment. His technology is second to none and his laser beam is all-powerful. Look out, baddies, Robo Man's in town!

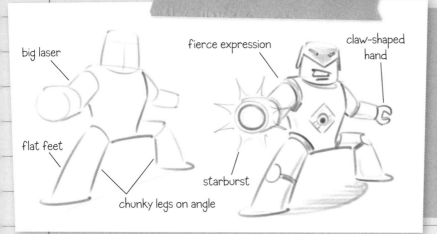

big laser

fierce expression

claw-shaped hand

flat feet

starburst

chunky legs on angle

477   Shadow Girl

Shadow Girl creeps around in the shadows in her dark suit, prowling the city skyline like a cat in the night. She's lightning quick with her trusty golden lasso.

curly hair

loopy lasso

dark shading

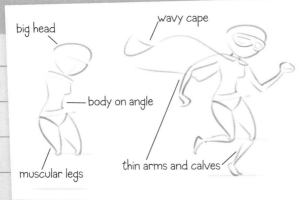

big head

wavy cape

body on angle

muscular legs

thin arms and calves

478

Secret agent

He may look like your everyday businessman, but he's on a special mission to save the world. Turn around and in a split second, he'll be gone!

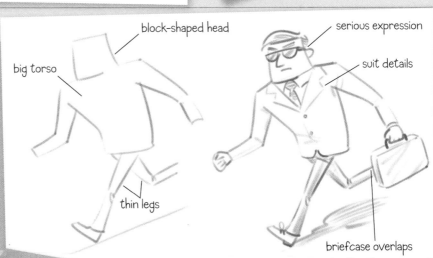

block-shaped head

serious expression

big torso

suit details

thin legs

briefcase overlaps

Girl squad

These secret agents are gorgeous, cool and not to be messed with! To draw the girl squad, you must start with their skeletons. In the first step, observe how each of their bodies is made up of a face cross, lines and shapes. These girls are full of energy – the angle of their skeletons and the positioning of their limbs set up their action poses. In the second step, their forms are built around the skeletons.

spine on angle

hips on angle

A-shaped legs

facing forward

curved spine

bent legs

shoulders on angle

short spine

leg and arm cross over

479

480

481

wavy hair

curved chest

arm behind

fierce expression

straight arm

arm behind

angry expression

hair moves

arm behind

482 Robin Hood

Robbing from the rich to help the poor, Robin is coming to your hood to save the day. His super-sharp archery skills have the bad guys shaking in their boots. Look at that perfectly straight arm!

bow lines up

looking left

straight shoulders

straight-arm pose

spine on angle

chiselled jaw

kneeling

483 Warrior princess

This Amazonian woman is powerful and has awesome fighting skills. As well as being beautiful, she is a fearsome warrior who has a reputation for winning battles.

fierce expression

sticks on same angle

fiery hair

straight arm

angled shoulders

straight thigh

curved boot

484 Tarzan

Tarzan was orphaned in the jungle at a young age. He was raised by animals, and developed amazing strength and agility from swinging on vines in the jungle. Tarzan loves to save damsels in distress.

long, wavy hair

muscular form

body on angle

holding onto vine

BUST A MOVE

Get off the couch and get your body moving! Wrestle an opponent, lift some weights or climb a mountain. Nothing is out of reach when you're fighting fit and healthy. There are so many amazing things we can do with our bodies. Traceurs flip and bounce off buildings. Breakdancers spin on their heads. Wow! Don't you wish you could do that?

485 Kung-fu fighter

Kung-fu is a form of martial arts used for self-defence. It dates back thousands of years. It takes great discipline to master the skill of kung-fu. Ha! Take that!

1 Draw the boy's head, face cross and shoulder line. Add his curved chest then his elevated leg. Now add the leg bent behind.

2 Draw his hair and ears, then add his arms and hands. Notice how one hand forms a fist and the other is open. Draw his ankles and shoes.

3 Draw his fierce expression over the face cross. Draw the neckline of his jacket, then add his moving belt. Darken and define his outline then add soft shading. Is everyone ready for kung-fu fighting?

486

487

Kung-fu kids

These kids are showing us their classic kung-fu moves with great skill and concentration. The girl could flip you in the blink of an eye, and the boy could hold that pose for hours. The positioning of the hands and feet are the most important aspects of these drawings.

488

Sumo wrestler

This big, beefy wrestler has a giant stomach and shoulders and can certainly stand his ground. He looks pretty annoyed, so don't mess with him! He has a strong, square pose and his legs are wide apart.

hands on knees
square pose
bun hairdo
angry expression
legs wide apart
loincloth

489

Rock climber

One false move and it's goodbye, apple pie! Strong footholds and handholds are really important in this game, as is the right equipment. This rock climber is climbing a crevasse above a canyon. Don't look down!

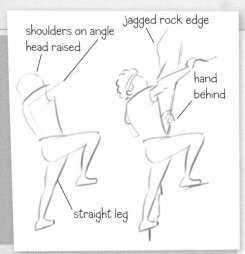

shoulders on angle
head raised
jagged rock edge
hand behind
straight leg

shading
climbing gear

 TIP Check out Facial Expressions on page 6 of the introduction to learn more about developing a character's emotion!

big jaw
cheesy expression
oversized muscles
tiny waist
muscle definition

490

Body builder

This body builder is a bit of a poser, showing off his moves along with his oversized chest and biceps. He's a bit out of proportion with his little legs!

491 Breakdancer

Breakdancing developed during the 1970s and has its roots in hip-hop culture. Breakdancers can perform all sorts of moves and tricks, including backspins, windmills and headspins. Show us your moves!

1 Draw the dancer's head and face cross followed by his shoulders and chest on an angle. Draw his arm with a flat hand shape. Add his pants, then his legs and feet.

2 Draw his cap on the side, then shape his arm and legs around the line work. Define his shoes and fingers. Add the other sleeve of his t-shirt.

3 Draw his face over the cross. Add the folds of his clothing. Darken and define his outline, then add the detailing of his shoes. Add soft shading and the shadow below. Get down to the beat!

492

493

B-boys

Check out these b-boys and their fancy moves. Their backs are curved and their legs are contorted and crossed. A single-handed handstand isn't easy. Don't try this at home!

494 Traceur

A traceur is someone who takes part in a sport called parkour. Parkour is a kind of urban acrobatics, where people flip and bound off obstacles such as buildings. What a wacky sport! It takes a lot of guts and determination to manipulate your body in this way, that's for sure!

face over cross

legs behind

leaning on ledge

495 Rollergirl

This girl's going for broke, speeding around the rink in her cool outfit. She's on a mission to win and will bump players off at any cost. Out of the way!

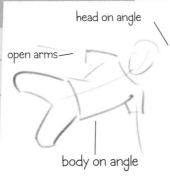

head on angle

open arms

body on angle

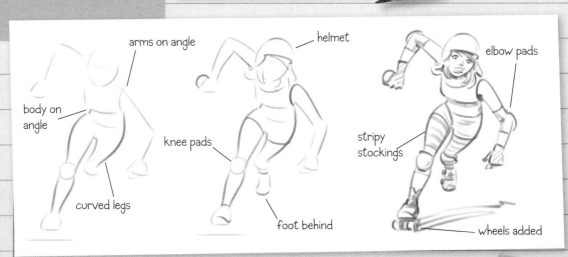

arms on angle

helmet

elbow pads

body on angle

knee pads

stripy stockings

curved legs

foot behind

wheels added

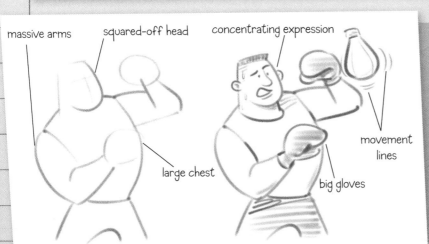

massive arms

squared-off head

concentrating expression

large chest

movement lines

big gloves

496

Boxer in training

He's practising for his next big fight and has nothing but winning on his mind. This big-chested, muscly boxer thinks he's the greatest. He's working up a sweat. Time to get in the ring, muscle man!

SHOWTIME

Roll up, roll up! It's showtime! Look at the trapeze artist soaring across the big top. Light the fuse – the human cannonball is ready to be fired from the cannon. The acrobats are balancing on the highwire as the audience oohs and aahs. Look how many balls that clown can juggle! Ladies and gentlemen, welcome to the circus!

497 Unicyclist

This lady must have an extreme level of skill to multitask like that! Look at her, balancing precariously on her unicycle while spinning hoops around her limbs. Who knows how she actually does it?

1 Draw the lady's head shape followed by her chest and her front leg. Draw the unicycle's seat and pole under her bottom, then add the oval wheel. Add the other leg behind.

2 Draw her open arms with her palms facing up. Add a curved neckline to her costume and draw the outline of her skirt.

3 Draw her smiley face and the bumpy outline of her curly hair. Lightly draw two hoops on each arm and on her leg. Add a frilly skirt and the stripes on her stockings. Define her boot, then add the pedals, spokes and tyre. Once you add soft shading, she's ready to roll.

498

Trapeze artists

Swinging high in the big top, these two trapeze artists mirror each other's movements, but differ in their costumes. There is great symmetry in this scene!

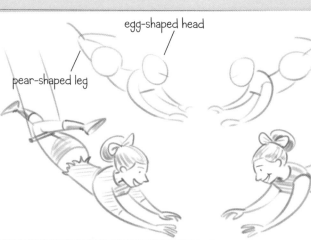

egg-shaped head

leg bends over

pear-shaped leg

leg straight behind

499
Highwire balancing act

How does he do it? Walking carefully across the highwire, showing great poise and balance, this acrobat is a master of his craft. Dressed in lycra and holding a long pole across his body, will he make it to the end?

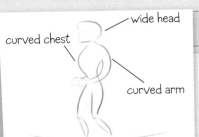

curved chest
wide head
curved arm

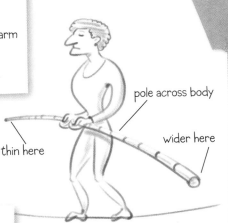

pole across body
thin here
wider here

500
Human cannonball

Being shot out of a cannon? This guy must be crazy! The force of the gunpowder sends him straight up and out. Who knows where he'll end up?

bottle-top shape on an angle
shooting straight

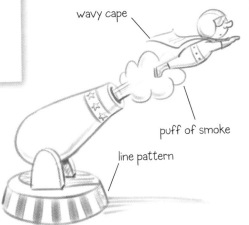

wavy cape
puff of smoke
line pattern

501
Juggling clown

Send in the clowns! Clowns may look unusual with their big red noses, oversized shoes and strange make-up, but they sure are funny! They make us laugh with goofy acts and juggling tricks.

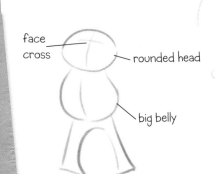

face cross
rounded head
big belly
puffy hair
looking up
big sleeves
oversized shoes
open hands

hinkler

Published by Hinkler Books Pty Ltd
45–55 Fairchild Street
Heatherton Victoria 3202 Australia
www.hinkler.com.au

© Hinkler Books Pty Ltd 2012, 2014

Illustrator: Paul Könye
Author: Kate Ashforth
Cover design: Ginny Wescott
Cover and section openers illustrator: Heath McKenzie
Layout: Lisa Howard
Prepress: Graphic Print Group

Pencils © Iwona Grodzka/shutterstock.com
Striped notebook paper texture © WimL/shutterstock.com
Strips of masking tape © M.E. Mulder/shutterstock.com

The drawings in this book are cartoons and caricatures, in which a
subject's features or characteristics are exaggerated for comic effect.
No offence is intended to any persons, living or dead.

ISBN: 978 1 7436 3545 2

Printed and bound in China